Achieving Creative Justice in the U.S. Creative Sector

Caste and the discrimination, exclusion, marginalization, othering, oppression, subalterning, and subjugation that it produces continue to challenge creative industries compromising culture's verisimilitude as a public good. *Achieving Creative Justice in the U.S. Creative Sector* explores the relationships between access diversity, equity, and inclusion (ADEI) and *creative justice* in the U.S. creative sector as *a* solution to meaningfully address enduring creative *in*justices.

Whether it's the #BlackLivesMatter, #LandBack, or #MeToo movements, caste remains structurally and systemically built into U.S. Society and thereby the creative sector. Acknowledging this realization after George Floyd's murder in 2020 has galvanized a quest for solutions. This book encourages sincere consideration for the human toll of insisting on artistic excellence and artistic merit at the expense of profound and unnecessary identity-based human suffering.

Providing a practical guide on how to activate ADEI to achieve *creative justice* and a research agenda, this book is an essential reading for practitioners and scholars who feel compelled to address creative *in*justices that constrain the creative flourishing of historically and continuously low casted peoples throughout the entire cultural ecosystem that defines the U.S. creative sector.

antonio c. cuyler is Professor of Music in Entrepreneurship and Leadership and Faculty Associate in Voice and Opera in the School of Music, Theatre & Dance (SMTD), and Faculty Associate in the African Studies Center at the University of Michigan. His Black-owned arts consultancy, Cuyler Consulting, LLC, partners with cultural organizations to maximize their performance and community relevance through access, diversity, equity, and inclusion (ADEI).

Routledge Focus on the Global Creative Economy

Series Editor

Aleksandar Brkić

Goldsmiths, University of London, UK

This innovative Shortform book series aims to provoke and inspire new ways of thinking, new interpretations, emerging research, and insights from different fields. In rethinking the relationship of creative economies and societies beyond the traditional frameworks, the series is intentionally inclusive. Featuring diverse voices from around the world, books in the series bridge scholarship and practice across arts and cultural management, the creative industries and the global creative economy.

Creative Work Beyond Precarity
Learning to Work Together
Tim Butcher

Youth Culture and the Music Industry in Contemporary Cambodia
Questioning Tradition
Darathtey Din

Global Crisis and the Creative Industries
Analysing the Impact of the Covid-19 Pandemic
Ryan Daniel

Creative Economy and Sustainable Development
The Context of Indian Handicrafts
Madhura Dutta

Achieving Creative Justice in the U.S. Creative Sector
antonio c. cuyler

For more information about this series, please visit: www.routledge.com/Routledge-Focus-on-the-Global-Creative-Economy/book-series/RFGCE

Achieving Creative Justice in the U.S. Creative Sector

antonio c. cuyler

Routledge
Taylor & Francis Group
LONDON AND NEW YORK

First published 2025
by Routledge
4 Park Square, Milton Park, Abingdon, Oxon OX14 4RN

and by Routledge
605 Third Avenue, New York, NY 10158

Routledge is an imprint of the Taylor & Francis Group, an informa business

This book is freely available in an open-access edition thanks to TOME (Toward an Open Monograph Ecosystem)—a collaboration of the Association of American Universities, the Association of University Presses, and the Association of Research Libraries—and the generous support of the University of Michigan's College of Literature, Science & the Arts and the Office of the Vice President for Research. Learn more at the TOME website, available at: openmonographs.org

British Library Cataloguing-in-Publication Data
A catalogue record for this book is available from the British Library

Library of Congress Cataloging-in-Publication Data
Names: Cuyler, Antonio C. (Antonio Christopher), 1978– author
Title: Achieving creative justice in the U.S. creative sector / antonio c.cuyler.
Description: Abingdon, Oxon ; New York, NY : Routledge, 2025. | Series: Routledge focus on the global creative economy | Includes bibliographical references and index.
Identifiers: LCCN 2024057926 (print) | LCCN 2024057927 (ebook) | ISBN 9781032160535 hardback | ISBN 9781032160542 paperback | ISBN 9781003246909 ebook
Subjects: LCSH: Cultural industries—United States | Social justice—United States | Marginality, Social—United States | Caste—United States
Classification: LCC HD9999.C9473 U63 2025 (print) | LCC HD9999.C9473 (ebook) | DDC 306.0973—dc23/eng/20250305
LC record available at https://lccn.loc.gov/2024057926
LC ebook record available at https://lccn.loc.gov/2024057927

ISBN: 978-1-032-16053-5 (hbk)
ISBN: 978-1-032-16054-2 (pbk)
ISBN: 978-1-003-24690-9 (ebk)

DOI: 10.4324/9781003246909

Typeset in Times New Roman
by Apex CoVantage, LLC

To the U.S. creative sector whose full power, unfortunately, remains constrained by the absurdity and insidiousness of caste and the discrimination, exclusion, marginalization, oppression, othering, subalterning, and subjugation that it produces.

Contents

List of Illustrations

Figures

Tables

Acknowledgments

I began thinking about ‘Creative Justice’ in 2017 after Dr. Melissa Nisbett suggested that I read Dr. Mark Banks’ *Creative Justice: Cultural Industries, Work and Inequality* at the Brokering Intercultural Exchange Network in Zürich, Switzerland. I remain grateful to Dr. Nisbett for her suggestion. I am also grateful to Dr. Banks for his work, which has impaled my own on the topic. Lastly, I am grateful for the many artists, colleagues, creatives, cultural organizations, cultural workers, and scholars who have afforded me voluminous opportunities to refine my thinking about ‘Creative Justice’ and how the U.S. creative sector might achieve it.

1 Caste in U.S. Society and the Creative Sector

In the 1960 essay, "History Is a Weapon They Can't Turn Back", James Baldwin said, "It took many years of vomiting up all of the filth I'd been taught about myself, and half believed, before I was able to walk on the earth as though I had a right to be here". I highlight this quote here at the beginning of Chapter 1 as a precursor to my discussion of the evolution, history, and origin of the United States of America (U.S.), which remains tethered to profound identity-based human suffering. The country's history began with European colonizers murdering Indigenous peoples and illegally, immorally, and unethically possessing their lands under the guise of religious freedom (Peck, 2021). Too many stories exist about the cruelties that Indigenous peoples have and continue to endure due to colonizers. Yet, the mischaracterizations about the relationships between Indigenous and non-Indigenous peoples through Thanksgiving, a U.S. national holiday, offer a poignant case to interrogate the relationships between Indigenous peoples and the U.S.

In *Time*, Brian Weeden, the chairman of the Mashpee Wampanoag, stated,

> I personally think that it's just another reminder of all the horrible things that this nation has done to not only us, but all Native people. For this nation to right a lot of their wrongs, they're gonna have to own up to their racism, which they don't want to do.

Though the Mashpee Wampanoag saved Europeans from death, the colonizers re-paid their altruism with murder, theft, and violence. Today, the tribe possesses only half of 1% of their ancestral land (Waxman, 2021). Furthermore, Koch et al. (2019) argued that global warming began with the mass genocide of Indigenous peoples in the 1500s.

Then, in 1619, colonizing Europeans abducted and in bondaged Angolan Africans, implicating them, and other west Africans, in their crimes against Indigenous peoples for almost 250 years (Winfrey et al., 2023). I consider the Trans-Atlantic Slave Trade a cultural policy worthy of much more scholarly attention because of the ways in which it simultaneously constrained and enabled the cultural engagement, practices, and values of people of

DOI: 10.4324/9781003246909-1

African descent on the continent and across the diaspora (cuyler, 2022b; cuyler, 2023b; Saha, 2018). Though the U.S. constitution abolished slavery in 1865 after the civil war, Mississippi only ratified the 13th amendment on February 7, 2013 (Nuwer, 2013).

As evidence of slavery's enduring legacy in the U.S. today, Lasseter et al. (2023) found that more than 100 governors, justices, lawmakers, and presidents have slaveholding ancestors, including the first Biracial president of the U.S., Barack Obama. Despite their post-slavery plight in the U.S., the descendants of in bondaged Africans have always creatively resisted their caste (cuyler, 2023b). For example, Hinton (2021) revealed that on December 17, 1951, William Patterson and Paul Robeson submitted a bold petition to the United Nations (UN) accusing the U.S. of genocide against Black people. At the time, the word "genocide" was only seven years old, had been coined during World War II in a book about Nazi atrocities, and adopted by the United Nations in 1948. Ironically, Hitler sent Nazis to the U.S. to study how the U.S. subjugated Black people during Jim Crow so that he could replicate the practice on Jewish people (Peck, 2022; Wilkerson, 2020).

Nevertheless, the U.S.' outsized power in the UN obstructed Patterson and Robeson's efforts to attain accountability for the descendants of in bondaged Africans in the U.S. Only recently, with the country's global standing severely weakened by the election of its 45th president and the incessant murders of Black people during the COVID-19 pandemic did the Human Rights Watch finally declare, "the U.S.' historical and continuous treatment of Black people a crime against humanity" (Human Rights Watch, 2022). After the U.S. House of Representatives apologized for slavery in 2008 (Lewis, 2016), achieving reparations for the descendants of in bondaged Africans *in the U.S.*, unequivocally, remains the top priority and the second step in atonement for the grave crimes against humanity that the descendants of in bondaged Africans in the U.S. have and continue to suffer.

During the 2024 Presidential election cycle many Black people, especially Black men, who democrats have repeatedly disappointed, and for whom republicans remain a repugnant option, remained deeply dissatisfied with their political options (Hunnicutt & Renshaw, 2023). Black men have also expressed annoyance, exhaustion, and frustration at rhetoric asking them to, yet again, save a democracy that has historically and continuously disenfranchised them from the U.S.' multi-racial democratic experiment. Even when the descendants of in bondaged Africans have used power to force the U.S. to live up to its espoused principles of democracy (Hannah-Jones, 2019; Asare, 2022), the government remains recalcitrant to making the most just decisions due to White accommodationism and White appeasement (Floyd & cuyler, 2023). In addition, though 77% of Black Americans believe that the descendants of in bondaged Africans in the *U.S.* should receive reparations, only 18% of White Americans agreed (Blazina & Cox, 2022).

In the U.S., caste, manifested as racism, does not only affect Indigenous and peoples of African descent. Though the U.S. census counts Middle

Eastern and North African (MENA) Americans as White, they receive few of the same privileges as White Americans, especially because of their religious beliefs (Alsharif & Tensley, 2022). After 9/11, Arab Americans faced attacks, including the registry of Middle East-born males known as the National Security Entry-Exit Registration System (NSEERS) (Vartanian, 2020). MENA Americans endure unrelenting racialized microaggressions today because of the ongoing conflict between Hamas and Israel. This 'forever' conflict has also negatively impacted Jewish people, another low casted group of people in U.S. society, because of their ethnicity and religion. Indeed, reported incidents of anti-semitism have risen by 337% since the October 7, 2023, attack (Anti-Defamation League, 2023).

After the COVID-19 pandemic ensnared the world, Zheng and Zompetti (2023) argued that Asian Americans have increasingly experienced violent racist attacks encouraged by the 45th president's rhetoric. His rhetoric also inflamed relationships between the U.S. and Puerto Rico in the aftermath of Hurricane Maria. Furthermore, Hispanic/Latine Americans frequently face racialized microaggressions about their immigration status and assumptions that they take jobs from native-born workers (Leguizamo, 2018). However, immigrants greatly benefit the U.S. population and productivity growth. Immigrants receive patents at twice the rate of their native-born counterparts, and they have a complementary vital skillset (Edelberg & Dollar, 2023). Because all non-Indigenous peoples are immigrants due to settler colonialism, should Indigenous worldviews not inform all the U.S. government's immigration policies?

Though U.S. Civil Rights legislation aimed to eradicate it, racism remains so intractable in U.S. society that the American Public Health Association declared it a public health crisis in 2020. Perhaps they should have declared caste the public health crisis. Racism and White supremacy culture, ideological infectious diseases of caste, continue to plague U.S. society (Floyd & cuyler, 2023; Okun, 2021). Though Okun (2021) argued that White supremacy culture targets and violates people of the global majority and their communities with the intent to destroy them directly, Vice-President Kamala Harris, senator Tim Scott, presidential candidate Nikki Haley, and representative Jim Clyburn, among others, foolishly and recklessly say, "America is not a racist country" (Alfaro & Vazquez, 2024). In fact, Andrew Bates, the White House deputy press secretary, in reference to calling for the genocide of Jews, stated, "It's unbelievable that this needs to be said: calls for genocide are monstrous and antithetical to everything we represent as a country" (Paybarah & Alfaro, 2023). However, the five times that the U.S. government 'officially' apologized all relate to its historic and ongoing practice of racial caste (Lewis, 2016), which includes genocide, most recently the genocide of Palestinians. Because caste manifested itself as racialized capitalism through the Trans-Atlantic Slave Trade, the first global enterprise in human history, the phenomenon has remarkable implications not only for business in the U.S.

today, and specifically relative to accounting, financing, leadership, and management, but also for how U.S. society thinks about labor. But even racialized capitalism has its limits, if *not* adopting an anti-caste, and specifically an anti-racism, ethos, and practice cost the U.S. culturally, demographically, financially, politically, socially, and most importantly in terms of health.

As Becker (1971) theorized in *The Economics of Discrimination*, racism cost the U.S. economy **$51 trillion** from 1990 to 2019 (Buckman et al., 2021). Buckman et al. (2021) also indicated that ensuring that all citizens have an equitable opportunity to participate in the economy is an economically significant way to increase aggregate prosperity. But do enough White Americans care, especially when the system incentivizes their fealty to it through material gain? As a high casted group, do they know that, as Metzl (2019) and Case and Deaton (2020) argued, too many of them die of Whiteness?

In addition to racism, poverty remains astoundingly engineered by the U.S. government. Approximately, 37.9 million or 11.6% of the population lived in poverty in 2021 (United States Census Bureau, 2023). In 2023, across the country workers engaged in strikes in industries as diverse as automotives, entertainment, healthcare, hospitality, and museums because those who have amassed unimaginable wealth do not feel compelled to share the fruits of that wealth equitably with their employees who labored to create it. Desmond (2023) identified mis-informed policy decisions, the greed of the privileged, and their ability to influence policy as explanations for why far too many U.S. citizens wade unnecessarily in grueling poverty. Alas, too many people believe that someone must live on the bottom of the social rung of society.

Caste and the discrimination, exclusion, marginalization, oppression, othering, subalterning, and subjugation that it produces impact other groups based on their social identities in the U.S., too (Wilkerson, 2020). As though people with disabilities did not exist before 1990, in that year, the U.S. government finally passed the *Americans with Disabilities Act* (ADA), but without a regulatory agency to investigate and act on disability-based claims of discrimination. Albert Dytch has filed more than 180 ADA lawsuits to signal this regulatory need to the government (Markham, 2021). Approximately 7% of U.S. citizens identified as bisexual, gay, or lesbian (Brown, 2023). However, the census does not acknowledge them even though the government uses it to inform its funding priorities and policy decisions. Those minoritized because of their affectional orientation receive little to no consideration in funding and policy discourses at the federal level. This may help to explain why the government has not passed the *Equality Act*, which would include national nondiscrimination protections for this low casted group of tax-paying citizens. But also, White Christian nationalists impose their values and will on society without having the moral authority to do so (Smietana, 2023).

White Christian nationalists claim to care about protecting children from drag queens and all manner of threats, but they lack the decisive ethical and moral courage to protect children from the threats that exist within their own ranks. The catholic, evangelical, and southern Baptist churches continue to grapple with massive sexual abuse and assault scandals (Silk, 2022). In addition, conservatives aim to ban all abortions nationally, while refusing to protect children from mass shootings in schools (Stewart, 2023). Observing this phenomenon in U.S. society begs the question, how would young activists fare in court if they sued their city, county, state, and national governments for a dereliction of duty in protecting their life, liberty, and pursuit of happiness? In addition, a recent study found that "White Christians believe that claims of nonexistent racial discrimination remain a bigger problem than actual racism" (Hurst, 2023).

The government has yet to ratify the *Equal Rights Act*, which would ban discrimination and harassment inflicted upon women. This includes a person's rights to choose how 'they' manage 'their' pregnancy with 'their' doctor. Furthermore, caste compounds based on the intersectionality of peoples' social identities (Crenshaw, 1989). U.S. policy and practice have yet to prioritize addressing this reality ethically, legally, materially, morally, or practically. Unless one has "high caste in spades" based on their identities as abled-bodied, middle-aged or above, Christian, cisgender, heterosexual, male, middle class or above, and White, one will inevitably experience identity-based human suffering in the U.S. This identity-based human suffering typically requires the additional burden of emotional and intellectual labor navigating societal systems intended to constrain their flourishing and thriving. What would the country's trajectory have been if it had been the founding 'people', instead of the 'founding fathers?' Did hubris undermine the U.S. evolution from the start because of a lack of real diversity, equity, and inclusion? Still, some politicians privileged by sharing the 'founding fathers' social identities as high casted espouse and practice grievance politics alleging 'reverse discrimination' and 'replacement theory', which continue to embolden many social phenomena, among them including the January 6 insurrection, a neo-civil and cultural war, and the murders of the descendants of in bondaged Africans and other peoples.

Given the quotient of their compounded high caste in the U.S., why are most mass shooters cis, White, men, and considered 'mentally' unstable? Why are most victims of gun suicide White men (Metzl, 2019; Case & Deaton, 2020)? Is the weight of cis, White, maleness too much to bear, and the unearned high caste that it produces an existential threat agitated by proactive attempts to course correct for centuries of caste? Okun (2021) warned that White supremacy culture targets and violates White people with a persistent invitation to collude that will inevitably destroy their humanity. At the same time, the Republican party has efficiently automated negative, reactive, and revenge policy responses to alleged grievances in states dominated by a Grand Old Party (GOP) electoral supermajority.

Governor Ron DeSantis, as an example, signed the *STOP Wrongs to Our Kids and Employees* (WOKE) Act into law in 2022 making it more difficult to address enduring structural and systemic caste in Florida. This schizophrenic and vague legislation prohibits instruction on race relations or diversity that implies a person's status as either privileged or oppressed is necessarily determined by his or her race, color, national origin, or sex (Riley, 2022). It also fails miserably at trying to legislate feelings by enshrining White people's emotional immaturity into law by keeping them from feeling guilt, remorse, and shame about how they have also been casted historically and continuously to benefit materially from their ancestors' brutality, cruelty, inhumanity, and savagery. Yet, their fear, guilt, and shame must not stop and/or undermine progress on addressing this wrong, eradicating caste, and manifesting long-awaited justice.

Though support for the #BlackLivesMatter movement increased globally immediately following George Floyd's murder, less than 10% of White citizens admitted to carrying guilt about Black suffering (National Public Radio, 2021) compelling me to wonder, where exactly, is this prodigious outpouring of White guilt the Republicans have sought to eradicate through reactive policymaking? Also, if there is so much White guilt, why do so few White Americans support reparations for the descendants of in bondaged Africans *in the U.S.*? In Florida, when asked by a judge to define 'woke' during the three-day trial challenging the suspension of Andrew Warren, a Democratic state attorney who signed a pledge against prosecuting abortion-related cases, the governor's counsel described it as, "it would be the belief there are systemic injustices in American society and the need to address them" (Rohrer, 2022). It would have made for a more interesting case if the judge had asked the governor and his counsel to prove beyond a reasonable doubt that systemic injustices do not exist in U.S. society. Hashtag activism, as one indicator, enabled by social media, including #BlackLivesMatter, #KnowYourStatus, #LandBack, #MeToo, #StopAsianHate, #StopPoverty, #TransIsBeautiful, and #Unhoused, suggests a wretched reality that unearned advantages obstruct the highest casted people in the U.S. from seeing.

Furthermore, a gerontocracy across the executive, judicial, and legislative branches of government has broken the implicit social contract with middle-aged leadership by incessantly subverting the peaceful transfer of power among generations (Smith, 2023). While some Gen X and millennial political leaders flirt with authoritarianism, demagoguery, and fascism, too, (Riley, 2022; Rohrer, 2022), uncannily, the septuagenarian current president led the 2021 insurrection against the U.S. government. The gerontocracy, to which the 45th, 46th, and 47th presidents of the U.S. belong, also aided the rise of a hyper-conservative Supreme Court of the U.S. (SCOTUS) that overturned abortion rights, banned affirmative action in higher education, struck down student loan debt relief, and undermined the separation between church and state by permitting a Christian wedding photographer to preemptively discriminate against same-gender loving couples, and a host of decisions that do not reflect the desires of most citizens. SCOTUS 'constitutional originalists' have conveniently forgotten that colonizing and enslaving settlers fled Europe in search of religious freedom. While the

Court's ethics and legitimacy remain in question (Associated Press, 2023), how can a civil society compel social cohesion when its Supreme Court refuses to uphold the rule of law or hold itself accountable through a code of ethics? Perhaps the people, like the presidency, could constrain Congress and SCOTUS from hoarding power through term limits, but Congress itself would need to muster the moral courage to implement such an act.

In addition, though the electorate prefered to move on from gerontocratic presidential candidates (Lerer & Epstein, 2023), the formerly known as "law and order" party selected a candidate found liable of sexual abuse, convicted of 34 counts of fraud, twice impeached, and faced three additional indictments on alleged criminal activity (Hubbard, 2023), one including accusations that he led an insurrection against the U.S. government, even though the U.S. constitution clearly stated,

> No person shall be a Senator or Representative in Congress, or elector of President and Vice-President, or hold any office, civil or military, under the United States, or under any State, who, having previously taken an oath, as a member of Congress, or as an officer of the United States, or as a member of any State legislature, or as an executive or judicial officer of any State, to support the Constitution of the United States, shall have engaged in insurrection or rebellion against the same, or given aid or comfort to the enemies thereof. But Congress may by a vote of two-thirds of each House, remove such disability.
>
> (U.S. Senate, 2023)

Though he ultimately relinquished his bid (Robinson, 2024), President Biden's ego and stubbornness made him feel entitled to a second term while ignoring that his 36 years in the senate, 8 years as vice-president, and 4 years as president also made him a political liability to the same democracy that he claimed to want to save. In 48 years of public service, why did he not advocate for codifying *Roe v. Wade* or affirmative action into law? Most importantly, to the chagrin of U.S. democracy, why has he and his party struggled to pass legislation that would make voting a constitutional right for all citizens, including convicted felons? Given this current situation, has the U.S. been *playing* or *practicing* democracy? Nevertheless, even if 67% of eligible voters cast more ballots in the 2020 election, democracy cannot thrive when the government has effectively disenfranchised nearly 80 million people, or a third of the eligible electorate from voting (Montanaro, 2020), can it?

Humans designed the 'system' that those living in the U.S. today inherited to produce inequitable outcomes for other humans based on their caste. Inspired by Wilkerson (2020), Adams et al. (2022), and the National Museum of African American History and Culture (2023), Table 1.1 presents social identities, the low casted groups, the high casted groups, the type of privilege, form of caste that they experience, and the remedy for that form of caste.

Table 1.1 The Matrix of Caste in the U.S.

Social Identity	*Low Casted Group*	*High Casted Group*	*Privilege*	*Form of Caste*	*Remedy (Anti-caste)*
Ability	People w/Disabilities	Temporarily Able-bodied	Able-bodied Privilege	Ableism	Anti-ableism
	People considered unattractive	Attractive People	Beauty/ Pretty Privilege	Lookism	Anti-lookism
				Sizeism	Anti-sizeism
Affectional Orientation	Bi, Gay, Lesbian, Queer, Same Gender Loving (SGL)+	Straight People	Hetero Privilege	Heterosexism	Anti-heterosexism
Age	Mature & Young People	Mature & Young People	Age Privilege	Adultism	Anti-adultism
				Ageism	Anti-ageism
Class	Poor People	Wealthy People	Class Privilege	Classism	Anti-classism
U.S. Citizens	Immigrants	People who speak English	Native Privilege	Nativism	Anti-nativism
	Rural	People born in the U.S.	Geographic Privilege	Placism	Anti-placism
		People who live in cities and the suburbs			
Gender	Nonbinary, trans, & women	Cisgendered People & Men	Cis Privilege	Cisgenderism	Anti-cisgenderism
			Male Privilege	Sexism	Anti-sexism
Political Party Affiliation	Green Party, Independent, Libertarian, Non-affiliate	Democrats & Republicans	Political Party Privilege	Tribalism	Anti-tribalism
Race	People W/Darker Skin Complexions & People of the Global Majority	White People	White Privilege	Colorism	Anti-Colorism
				Racism	Anti-racism
Religion	Agnostics, Atheists, Hindus, Jews, Muslims, Santeríans, Wiccans, & others	Christians	Christian Privilege	Anti-semitism	Anti-religious oppression
				Islamophobia	
				Religious Oppression	

Diversity, Equity, and Inclusion as a Solution to Caste in the U.S.

In the *Cycle of Socialization*, Harro (2008) theorized the ways in which individuals internalize their roles in the *Matrix of Caste in the U.S.* through their interactions with family, government, institutions, media, and schools from birth. She also explained how people respond to this historical and contemporary context based on the quotient of their low casted and high casted social identities. Her counter-model, the *Cycle of Liberation*, offered suggestions for how individuals can challenge and change oppressive actions and relationships, particularly as a "cardiologist, endocrinologist, obesity specialist, health economist, and social epidemiologist all said versions of the same thing: striving to get ahead in an unequal society contributes to people in the United States aging quicker, becoming sicker and dying younger" (Johnson & Gomez, 2023; Diamond, 2023).

In the U.S., diversity, equity, and inclusion (DEI) aimed to not only aid compliance with the new Civil Rights legislation passed and enacted in the 1960s but also compel corporations, government, institutions, and organizations to change behaviors deeply rooted in systemic caste. Anand and Winters (2008) observed that DEI training evolved from compliance-oriented content (mid-1960s–early 1980s) to improving working relationships (mid-1980s to mid-1990s) to a more recent focus on accepting and leveraging all dimensions of diversity based on the belief that enhanced performance would result. U.S. society has realized that representation alone could and would not address the systemically embedded caste to which it socialized people without adding attention to equity and inclusion to transform the culture enabled by social norms.

Though aspects of DEI have broadly worked, caste remains an intractable characteristic of U.S. society. In April 2024, the *New York Times* reported on a study conducted by economists on 97 of the largest corporations in the U.S. Using fake resumes, the study revealed that some corporations chose not to interview applicants with "Black" names even though they had the same exact resume as applicants with "White" names. Relative to age, gender, and LGBTQ+ status, on average applicants did not treat female and male applicants differently, except for when it came to recruiting workers in traditionally gendered jobs. For example, female applicants received more call backs for jobs at Ann Taylor while male-identifying applicants received more callbacks for manufacturing jobs with Builders FirstSource. An intersectionality analysis revealed that a small benefit accrued to White female applicants, and a slight penalty existed for Black female applicants. The researchers also found a slight penalty for applicants over age 40. The researchers found no penalty for using nonbinary pronouns but identifying as gay through membership in an LGBTQ+ club on the résumé resulted in a slight penalty for White applicants but benefited Black applicants. Most importantly, the study's results showed a critical correlation that "more profitable companies remain less biased" (Kline et al., 2024; Miller & Katz, 2024).

But what exactly drives people in U.S. society to maintain an inherited system that fundamentally believes that identity-based human suffering is absolutely necessary? Furthermore, what compels leaders, political and otherwise, to engage in performative identity politics to inflict unnecessary identity-based suffering on other humans? According to Dr. Gwendolyn Keita, categorizing people and objects remains a natural human motivation. Discrimination, and I would argue, caste, goes beyond this natural practice of human sensemaking of people and objects.

> Research shows that the attitudes of people who discriminate reflect their history, sociocultural practices, economic forces, sociological trends, and the influence of community and family beliefs. Discrimination, and caste result from deep-seated and destructive generalizations about certain groups of people. In these cases, people harbor unrealistic, disparaging beliefs about a group and its members, while also maintaining a sense of the moral or intellectual superiority of their own group. These humans remain consciously aware of their negative emotions toward members of the group, and intentionally avoid, disadvantage, and harm them.
>
> (American Psychological Association, 2016)

Furthermore, if adopting an anti-caste ethos and practice yields profitability and a healthier society, why does caste remain a defining characteristic of the U.S., an alleged capitalist country? What, specifically, do people gain by abandoning profitability to exploit the opportunity to caste another human being lower than themself?

Power

The pursuit, retention, and use of power motivate the crimes against humanity that systemic caste systematically produces (Wilkerson, 2020). Liu (2014) defined power as "the ability to have people do what you would have them to do". He identified six sources of civic power: (1) physical force, (2) wealth, (3) state action, (4) social norms, (5) ideas, and (6) numbers. In addition to these six sources of power, he articulated the three laws of power as: (1) power is never static, (2) power is like water in that it is always flowing and moving, and (3), which resonates with Crenshaw's intersectionality theory, is that power compounds. Simply put, power begets power.

Humans can attain personal and/or positional power. One receives positional power as authority granted to them for a leadership role that they adorn. The leader may attain this role in a civic and/or professional setting. But personal power yields a different quality of outcomes because it relies on a leader's ability, talent, and skill at compelling and motivating people to follow them based on their needs and personal relationships with that leader. Still, power, in and of itself, is neutral. It has no interest in bad or good; or right or wrong (cuyler 2023c). Humans use power to not only enable bad and/or good but also constrain bad and/or good.

Why the Creative Sector?

If people can transform the oppressive actions and relationships that the *Matrix of Caste in the U.S.* produces in U.S. society, as Harro (2008) argued, then the creative sector is well-positioned to aid the consciousness of those who remain asleep to the system in which they exist and the existential threat that it poses to humanity by constraining human flourishing. Although a debate exists about if change should happen at the individual or systems level, in my view, change must happen at both levels. Given that humans designed the systems under which U.S. society operate, if access diversity, equity, and inclusion (ADEI) transformed humans, then the systems that they design will also transform. But what exactly is that power? Furthermore, why must the U.S. creative sector wield that power ethically, justly, and morally to the benefit of those most disadvantaged by the *Matrix of Caste in the U.S.*? Though I have heard some people who work in and outside the U.S. creative sector say, "people who work in the arts aren't abusive, ableist, adultist, classist, racist, sexist, etc.", movies such as *Fame, Amadeus, Farinelli, Black Swan, Whiplash, Tár, Chevalier, Maestro*, and the TV series *Mozart in the Jungle* suggest otherwise revealing insights about the ways in which humans abuse and misuse power in the creative sector, and for what reasons. The news headlines highlighted in Table 1.2 also provide evidence that the creative sector, too, is not invulnerable to abuses and misuses of power.

As a reminder, Black and other people of the global majority shared their experiences with racism within the creative sector during the 2020 summer of racial discontent in mass (cuyler, 2022a, 2023a, 2023c, Floyd & cuyler, 2023). The creative sector, perhaps more than any other sector in the U.S., should take the social transformation imperative implicit in ADEI seriously because it wields the power to tell an infinite number of stories about what it means to live as a human, particularly in U.S. society. Telling the full and vast story of human existence is critical because research has shown that culture can aid peoples' development of parasocial relationships with people who do not share their affectional and racial identities (Bond, 2021; Cuadrado-García & Montoro-Pons, 2021; cuyler, 2023b). Furthermore, according to Americans for the Arts (2022), 73% of U.S. citizens believe that the arts "help me to understand other cultures better". In addition, 72% of U.S. citizens believe that the arts "unify communities regardless of age, ethnicity, and race", a perspective observed across all demographic and economic categories.

Table 1.2 Examples of Caste in the U.S. Creative Sector

Headlines	*Source*	*Date*
1. Seeking Pay Equity, Female Flutist Sues Boston Symphony Orchestra.	NPR	7/5/2018
2. Assaults in dressing rooms. Groping during lessons. Classical musicians reveal a profession rife with harassment.	Washington Post	7/26/2018
3. Union Says, Plácido Domingo Engaged in 'Inappropriate Activity'.	NPR	2/25/2020
4. Patron attacks the Detroit Symphony over 'offensive' season of Black composers, and the classical music world responded.	Classic FM	4/23/2021
5. Racism, Income Inequality, and Climate Change Are the Topics Americans Most Want Museums to Address, According to a New Survey.	Artnet news	11/24/2021
6. Chicago Museum Payroll Manager Accused of Stealing $2M.	Hyperallergic	1/19/2023
7. MoMA Apologizes for Kicking Out Black Artist From Installation.	Hyperallergic	3/29/2023
8. Conductor who allegedly slapped singer pulls out of all 2023 performances.	The Guardian	8/31/2023
9. Disney's Legal Woes Mount As Exec Notes 'Pay Equity Nightmare' in Unsealed Court Docs.	The Hollywood Reporter	12/15/2023
10. Activision Blizzard to pay roughly $50 million in California discrimination case settlement.	Los Angeles Time	12/15/2023
11. A Hidden Sexual-Assault Scandal at the New York Philharmonic.	Vulture	4/16/2024
12. A Black rising star lost his elite orchestra job. He won't go quietly.	Washington Post	5/24/2024
13. Kehinde Wiley's Accusers Respond to Concerns Over Canceled Museum Shows.	Hyperallergic	6/27/2024
14. Behind the Pageantry of Shen Yun.	New York Times	8/15/2024
15. 'Such an injustice': Protesters decry firing of Dallas Black Dance Theatre dancers	Dallas Morning News	8/17/2024

Most importantly, as Boal (1979) argued,

> Art is a form of knowledge: the artist, therefore, has the obligation of interpreting reality, making it understandable. But, if instead he limits himself to re-producing it, he will fail to comprehend it or to make it comprehensible. And the more reality and art tends to be identical, the more useless it will be for the latter. The criterion of similarity is the measure of inefficiency.
> (p. 171)

Thus, culture can do more than just show people who they have been and who they are. It can also show people who they can become. U.S. society needs the creative sector to take on this challenge by centering and prioritizing the *creative justice* of all historically and continuously low casted peoples as it works to eradicate caste and its constraints on human flourishing.

My Positionality

I first began practicing ADEI in 7th grade at Stambaugh Middle School in Auburndale, Florida. Even then, human suffering compelled me to identify the unnecessary barriers erected by people to stop other people from flourishing. This behavior, I now understand as caste, still troubles me.

Today, in U.S. society, my upper-middle-class status, command of English, education, gender identity, and citizenship position me as high casted. Simultaneously, my affectional orientation, (dis)abilities, political party affiliation, race, and religious identity position me as low casted. I am a proud descendant of in bondaged Africans, specifically, the Mbundu, Djola, Kpelle, Mandinka, Mende, and Temne peoples of present-day Angola, Guinea-Bissau, Liberia, Senegal, and Sierra Leone. I do not speak for all people of African descent, in bondaged in the U.S. or elsewhere. However, as a Black American, the U.S. has denied me the privilege of falling in love with it by incessantly breaking so many of its promises to me and people like me. Though I have consistently embodied and lived tokenization as the first Black male to graduate from the Lois Cowles Harrison Visual and Performing Arts Center in voice, to complete the Master of Arts degree in Arts Administration from the Florida State University (FSU) College of Music, to complete the Ph.D. in Art Education with a major in Arts Administration, to earn promotion and tenure in the Department of Education (first global majority person), to earn promotion and tenure in the discipline of arts administration, entrepreneurship, leadership, and management; I am a survivor of an abusive, sadistic, and toxic relationship with the country in which my mother birthed me and remain vexed by the question, "why do I stay?"

Professionally, I am a full professor with tenure at the University of Michigan, which engaged me through its Anti-Racism Hiring Initiative (ARHI). After the murders of Ahmaud Aubery, Breonna Taylor, George Floyd, and Tony McDade, I founded Cuyler Consulting, LLC, a 100% Black-owned arts consultancy that partners with cultural organizations to maximize their performance and community relevance through ADEI. My consultancy offers climate, culture, and people surveys; education and professional development; evaluation and research; and strategic planning *with* cultural organizations of all types. In addition to working with the American Choral Directors Association, Chorus America, Dance/USA, League of American Orchestras, and OPERA America, I have worked with museums, opera companies, and orchestras, as well as arts funders. I have also held other roles within the creative sector including as an arranger, arts administrator, classical music radio host, composer, intern, scholar, and singer.

My socialization (Harro, 2008) has implicated me in caste. At times, I have perpetuated White supremacy culture's harms knowingly and unknowingly (Bacon, 2024). Because of critical incidents that have awakened me to this harm (Harro, 2008), today I actively resist the ways that the system seeks to dehumanize me by making me a bot of its will to dehumanize myself and others. Now, I strive to live as a glitch within the system so that the outcome of my liberation is my complete and full re-humanization. I am not subjective as my embodied and lived experiences, personal and professional through participant observation, autoethnographically inform the insights, observations, positions, and perspectives that I share within this book.

Definitions and Key Terms

To aid in the acquisition of the knowledge contained within this book, I will use the following key terms throughout this book:

1. **Ableism** – disability-based human suffering.
2. **Access** – is the removal of all barriers to participation.
3. **Adultism** – age-based human suffering that impacts people younger than 40.
4. **Ageism** – age-based human suffering that impacts people 40 and above.
5. **Anti-caste** – is the elimination of identity-based human suffering.
6. **Caste** – is the human impulse to classify, create hierarchies of, and affix value to people based on their social identities. It typically results in identity-based human suffering to the detriment of human flourishing.
7. **Cisgenderism** – is a prejudice like racism and sexism. It denies, ignores, denigrates, or stigmatizes non-cisgender forms of expression, sexual activity, behavior, relationship, or community. Cisgenderism exists in everyone, transgender individuals as well as cisgender individuals alike, because almost everyone exists in a predominately cisgender society that has little or no positive recognition of non-cisgender behavior, identity, and/or experience (Urban Dictionary, 2021).
8. **Classism** – is class-based human suffering.
9. **Colorism** – is skin complexion-based human suffering.
10. **Creative Justice** – is the manifestation of all historically and continuously low caste peoples living creative and expressive lives on their own terms.
11. **Creative Sector** – is the for-profit and nonprofit industrial complex that enables an economy based on artistic expression, creativity, and innovation.
12. **Diversity** – is a qualitative and/or quantitative assessment of the intentional engagement of the vastness of human difference.
13. **Equity** – is fairness in addressing historic, continuous, and long-suffered inequality.
14. **Heterosexism** – is the assumption that heterosexuality is the social and cultural norm as well as the prejudiced belief that heterosexuals, or "straight" people, are socially and culturally superior to lesbian, gay, bisexual, transgender, two-spirit, and queer (LGBTTQ) people (Rainbow Resource Centre, 2012).
15. **Inclusion** – is belonging, the antithesis of exclusion.
16. **Intersectionality** – asserts that people are often disadvantaged by multiple sources of identity: their ability, affectional orientation, age, class, gender race, religion, and other social identities (Crenshaw, 1989, 2016).
17. **Lookism** – is looks-based human suffering.
18. **Nativism** – is native status-based human suffering.
19. **Racism** – is race-based human suffering.

20. **Religious oppression** – is the systematic and systemic mistreatment of an individual or a group of individuals as a response to their religious beliefs or affiliations or lack thereof (Raz, 2021).
21. **Sexism** – is sex-based human suffering.
22. **Sizeism** – is size- and weight-based human suffering.
23. **Tribalism** – is tribe (identity group, political party, otherwise)-based human suffering.

In this chapter, I described the cultural, historical, political, and social contexts in which the U.S. creative sector exists as I see it. I argued that an obsession with power enables and motivates how U.S. society socializes citizens into its cultural, historical, political, and social contexts, including by casting them into a systemic matrix based on their devalued and valued social identities. I also discussed the importance of addressing caste and the discrimination, exclusion, marginalization, oppression, and subjugation that it produces within the creative sector. I described my positionality and closed the chapter with a definition of key terms I will use throughout this book.

In Chapter 2, I propose ADEI and *creative justice* as *a* solution to address the enduring and wicked problem of caste within the U.S. creative sector. I also define these goals and practices, theorize the relationships that exist between them, and describe their relationship to *creative justice*. Lastly, I argue that ADEI are goals and practices in and of themselves that enable *creative justice*, the long-term goal for which the U.S. creative sector should strive to achieve.

References

Adams, M., Bell, L., Goodman, D., Shlasko, D., Briggs, R., & Pacheco, R. (2022). *Teaching for Diversity and Social Justice*. Routledge.

Alfaro, M., & Vazquez, M. (2024, January 18). Haley Sparks a 2024 Debate: Whether the U.S. Is (or Ever Was) a Racist Country. https://washingtonpost.com/politics/2024/01/18/haley-racism-america-presidential-election/

Alsharif, M., & Tensley, B. (2022, April 28). Why Arab and Arab Americans Feel Being Counted as White in the U.S. Doesn't Reflect Their Reality. https://cnn.com/2022/04/28/us/arab-american-heritage-month-race-deconstructed-newsletter/index.html

American Psychological Association. (2016). Discussing Discrimination. https://apa.org/topics/racism-bias-discrimination/keita

Americans for the Arts. (2022). 10 Reasons to Support the Arts in 2022. https://americansforthearts.org/node/166236

Anand, R., & Winters, M.-F. (2008). A Retrospective View of Corporate Diversity Training from 1964 to the Present. *Academy of Management Learning & Education*, *7*(3), pp. 356–372.

Anti-Defamation League. (2023, December 11). ADL Reports Unprecedented Rise in Anti-Semitic Incidents Post-October 7. https://adl.org/resources/press-release/adl-reports-unprecedented-rise-antisemitic-incidents-post-oct-7

Asare, J. (2022, October 7). Have We Been Wrongfully Vilifying DEI Training? *Forbes*. https://forbes.com/sites/janicegassam/2022/10/07/have-we-been-wrongfully-vilifying-dei-training/?sh=4af908d53b35
Bacon, P. (2024, February 6). We Are Seeing the Limits of Diversity. *The Washington Post*. https://washingtonpost.com/opinions/2024/02/06/equity-diversity-inclusion-progressivism-limits/
Baldwin, J. (1960). History Is a Weapon They Can't Turn Back. https://historyisaweapon.com/defcon1/baldwincantturnback.html
Becker, G. (1971). *The Economics of Discrimination*, 2nd Ed. University of Chicago Press.
Blazina, C., & Cox, K. (2022, November 28). Black and White Americans Are Far Apart in Their Views of Reparations for Slavery. https://pewresearch.org/short-reads/2022/11/28/black-and-white-americans-are-far-apart-in-their-views-of-reparations-for-slavery/
Boal, A. (1979). *Theatre of the Oppressed*. Pluto.
Bond, B. J. (2021). The Development and Influence of Parasocial Relationships With Television Characters: A Longitudinal Experimental Test of Prejudice Reduction Through Parasocial Contact. *Communication Research*, *48*(4), pp. 573–593.
Brown, A. (2023, June 23). 5 Key Findings About LGBTQ+ Americans. https://pewresearch.org/short-reads/2023/06/23/5-key-findings-about-lgbtq-americans/
Buckman, S., Daly, M., Choi, L., & Seitelman, L. (2021). The Economic Gains From Equity. https://brookings.edu/wp-content/uploads/2021/09/15985-BPEA-BPEA-FA21_WEB_Buckman-et-al.pdf
Case, A., & Deaton, A. (2020). *Deaths of Despair and the Future of Capitalism*. Princeton University Press.
Crenshaw, K. (1989). Demarginalizing the Intersection of Race and Sex: A Black Feminist Critique of Antidiscrimination Doctrine, Feminist Theory and Antiracist Politics. *University of Chicago Legal Forum*, (1), pp. 139–167.
Crenshaw, K. (2016). The Urgency of Intersectionality. *TEDWomen*. https://ted.com/talks/kimberle_crenshaw_the_urgency_of_intersectionality/discussion
Cuadrado-García, M., & Montoro-Pons, J. D. (2021). LGB's Arts Affinity: An Empirical Study of Theater Audiences Based on Motivations. *Journal of Homosexuality*, *69*(8), pp. 1322–1341.
cuyler, a. c. (2022a). Moving Beyond @Operaisracist: Exploring Blacktivism as a Pathway to Antiracism and Creative Justice in Opera. In D. Abfalter & R. Reitsamer (Eds.), *Music as Labour: Inequalities and Activism in the Past and Present* (pp. 204–218). Routledge.
cuyler, a. c. (2022b). *Arts Management, Cultural Policy, & the African Diaspora*. Palgrave Macmillan.
cuyler, a. c. (2023a). Access, Diversity, Equity, and Inclusion (ADEI) in Cultural Organizations: Challenges and Opportunities. In A. Rhine & J. Pension (Eds.), *Business Issues in the Arts* (pp. 83–104). Routledge.
cuyler, a. c. (2023b). Casualties of Exclusionary Cultural Policies: Exploring the Paradox of Black American Cultural Engagement. *Journal for Cultural Research*, *27*(1), pp. 23–37.

cuyler, a. c. (2023c). (Un)Silencing Blacktivism in Opera: An Interview With Quodesia Johnson About the Letter to the Opera Field from Black Administrators. In A. Bull & C. Scharff (Eds.), *Voices for Change in the Classical Music Profession* (pp. 255–266). Oxford University Press.

Desmond, M. (2023, March 9). Why Poverty Persists in America? https://nytimes.com/2023/03/09/magazine/poverty-by-america-matthew-desmond.html

Diamond, D. (2023, December 28). America Has a Life Expectancy Crisis. But It's Not a Political Priority. *The Washington Post*. https://washingtonpost.com/health/2023/12/28/life-expectancy-no-political-response/?utm_campaign=wp_post_most&utm_medium=email&utm_source=newsletter&wpisrc=nl_most

Edelberg, W., & Dollar, D. (2023). Why Immigrants Are America's Superpower. https://brookings.edu/articles/why-immigrants-are-americas-superpower/?utm_campaign=Brookings%20Brief&utm_medium=email&utm_content=265084686&utm_source=hs_email

Floyd, Q., & cuyler, a. c. (2023). The Death of White Supremacy in the US Creative Sector & Implications for Arts Management: A Critical Race Theory View. In Y. Jung, N. Vakharia, & M. Vecco (Eds.), *The Oxford Handbook of Arts and Cultural Management*. Oxford University Press.

Hannah-Jones, N. (2019, August 14). Our Democracy's Founding Ideas Were False When They Were Written. Black Americans Have Fought to Make Them True. *The New York Times*. https://nytimes.com/interactive/2019/08/14/magazine/black-history-american-democracy.html

Harro, B. (2008). Updated Version of Cycle of Liberation. In M. Adams, W. J. Blumenfield, R. Castenada, H. W. Hackman, M. L. Peters, & X. Zuniga (Eds.), *Readings for Diversity and Social Justice* (pp. 463–469). Routledge.

Hinton, A. (2021). 70 Years Ago, Black Activists Accused the U.S. of Genocide. They Should Have Been Taken Seriously. *Politico*. https://apple.news/AYUzDvemqR8yWQwPIoAPbzA

Hubbard, K. (2023, August 15). Explainer: Trump's Four Indictments. https://usnews.com/news/national-news/articles/2023-08-15/explainer-trumps-four-indictments

Human Rights Watch. (2022, August 8). Racial Discrimination in the United States. https://hrw.org/report/2022/08/08/racial-discrimination-united-states/human-rights-watch/aclu-joint-submission

Hunnicutt, T., & Renshaw, J. (2023, August 2). Some Black Men Lose Faith in Biden, Democrats in 2024. *Reuters*. https://reuters.com/world/us/some-black-men-lose-faith-biden-democrats-2024-2023-08-01/

Hurst, K. (2023, August 5). Americans Are Divided on Whether Society Overlooks Racial Discrimination or Sees It Where It Doesn't Exist. https://pewresearch.org/short-reads/2023/08/25/americans-are-divided-on-whether-society-overlooks-racial-discrimination-or-sees-it-where-it-doesnt-exist/

Johnson, A., & Gomez, C. (2023, October 17). Stress Is Weathering Our Bodies from the Inside Out. *The Washington Post*. https://washingtonpost.com/health/interactive/2023/stress-chronic-illness-aging/

Kline, P., Rose, E., & Walters, C. (2024). A Discrimination Report Card. The University of Chicago Becker Friedman Institute for Economics. https://bfi.uchicago.edu/insight/research-summary/a-discrimination-report-card/

Koch, A., Brierley, C., Maslin, M., & Lewis, S. (2019). Earth System Impacts of the European Arrival and Great Dying in the Americas After 1492. *Quaternary Science Reviews*, *207*(1), pp. 13–36.

Lasseter, T., Delevingne, L., Brice, M., Bryson, D., Brown, N., & Bergin, T. (2023, June 27). America's Family Secret. *Reuters*. https://reuters.com/investigates/special-report/usa-slavery-lawmakers/

Leguizamo, J. (2018). John Leguizamo's Latin History for Morons. https://netflix.com/title/80225421

Lerer, L., & Epstein, R. (2023, August 15). The Biden-Trump Rematch That Nobody Wants. *The New York Times*. https://nytimes.com/2023/08/14/us/politics/2024-trump-biden-rematch.html

Lewis, D. (2016, May 27). Five Times the United States Officially Apologized. *Smithsonian Magazine*. https://smithsonianmag.com/smart-news/five-times-united-states-officially-apologized-180959254/

Liu, E. (2014). *How to Understand Power* [Video]. Ted Conferences. https://ted.com/talks/eric_liu_how_to_understand_power?language=en

Markham, L. (2021, July 21). The Man Who Filed More Than 180 Disability Lawsuits: Is It Profiteering or Justice? *The New York Times*. https://nytimes.com/2021/07/21/magazine/americans-with-disabilities-act.html

Metzl, J. (2019). *Dying of Whiteness: How the Politics of Racial Resentment Is Killing America's Heartland*. Basic Books.

Miller, C., & Katz, J. (2024, April 8). What Researchers Discovered When They Sent 80, 000 Fake Résumés to U.S. Jobs. *The New York Times*. https://nytimes.com/2024/04/08/upshot/employment-discrimination-fake-resumes.html

Montanaro, D. (2020, December 15). Poll: Despite Record Turnout, 80 Million Americans Didn't Vote. Here's Why. *National Public Radio*. https://npr.org/2020/12/15/945031391/poll-despite-record-turnout-80-million-americans-didnt-vote-heres-why

National Museum of African American History and Culture. (2023). Social Identities and Systems of Oppression. https://nmaahc.si.edu/learn/talking-about-race/topics/social-identities-and-systems-oppression

National Public Radio (NPR). (2021, June 9). The Racial Reckoning That Wasn't. *NPR*. https://npr.org/transcripts/1004467239

Nuwer, R. (2013, February 20). Mississippi Officially Ratifies Amendment to Ban Slavery, 148 Years Late. *Smithsonian Magazine*. https://smithsonianmag.com/smart-news/mississippi-officially-ratifies-amendment-to-ban-slavery-148-years-late-21328041/

Okun, T. (2021). White Supremacy Culture. https://whitesupremacyculture.info/characteristics.html

Paybarah, A., & Alfaro, M. (2023, December 6). White House, Lawmakers Criticize University Leaders' Answers on Antisemitism. *Washington Post*. https://washingtonpost.com/politics/2023/12/06/white-house-university-presidents-antisemitism-genocide/

Peck, R. (2021). *Exterminate All the Brutes*. HBO TV Series. Retrieved January 8, 2023, from https://hbo.com/exterminate-all-the-brutes

Raz, S. (2021). Diversity and Social Justice - Faculty Guide (2021 Edition).

Riley, K. (2022, April 22). Florida's Governor Just Signed the 'Stop Woke Act.' Here's What It Means for Schools and Businesses. https://time.com/6168753/florida-stop-woke-law/

Robinson, E. (2024, July 22). Biden Did His Part. Now Here's the Next Step. *The Washington Post*. https://washingtonpost.com/opinions/2024/07/22/biden-democrats-nominate-harris/?utm_source=email&utm_medium=lifecycle&utm_campaign=engagement&utm_content=bidenopinions&topicFollow=CP-19

Rohrer, G. (2022, December 3). In Andrew Warren Suspension Trial, Gov. DeSantis Officials Answer: What Does 'Woke' Mean? *Florida Politics*. https://floridapolitics.com/archives/574045-in-andrew-warren-suspension-trial-gov-desantis-officials-answer-what-does-woke-mean/

Saha, A. (2017). *Race and the Cultural Industries*. Wiley.

Silk, M. (2022, May 25). The Southern Baptist and Catholic Sexual Abuse Crises, Compared. https://religionnews.com/2022/05/25/comparing-the-southern-baptist-and-catholic-sexual-abuse-crises/

Smietana, B. (2023, January 10). Who Are the Christian Nationalists? A Taxonomy for the Post-January 6 World. *The Washington Post*. https://washingtonpost.com/religion/2023/01/06/christian-nationalism-groups/

Smith, D. (2023, February 19). Gerontocracy: The Exceptionally Old Political Class That Governs the U.S. *Guardian*. https://theguardian.com/us-news/2023/feb/19/us-congress-presidency-gerontocracy

Stewart, J. (2023, March 3). Interview with Oklahoma State Sen. Nathan Dahm. *The Problem*. https://youtube.com/watch?v=tCuIxIJBfCY

United States Census Bureau. (2023). National Poverty in America Awareness Month: January 2023. https://census.gov/newsroom/stories/poverty-awareness-month.html

United States Senate. (2023). Landmark Legislation: The Fourteenth Amendment. https://senate.gov/about/origins-foundations/senate-and-constitution/14th-amendment.htm#:~:text=Passed%20by%20the%20Senate%20on,laws%2C%E2%80%9D%20extending%20the%20provisions%20of

Urban Dictionary. (2021). Cisgenderism. https://www.urbandictionary.com/define.php?term=Cisgenderism

Vartanian, H. (2020, September 10). It's Time to End the 9/11 Tribute in Light. https://hyperallergic.com/587462/turning-off-the-tribute-in-light/?utm_medium=email&utm_campaign=W123023&utm_content=W123023+CID_9a38f64bc44d84eab237695f638d84bc&utm_source=hn&utm_term=register

Waxman, O. (2021). What Thanksgiving Means Today to the Native American Tribe That Fed the Pilgrims. *Time*. https://apple.news/A9yP-Z_j0SmCoA5w9nNUqqg

Wilkerson, I. (2020). *Caste: The Origins of Our Discontent*. Random House.

Winfrey, O., Jones, N., Guy, S., Williams, R., Lingo, K., & Roper, C. (2023). *The 1619 Project*. Hulu. https://press.hulu.com/shows/the-1619-project/

Zheng, J., & Zompetti, J. (2023). 'I'm Not a Virus': Asian Hate in Donald Trump's Rhetoric. *Asian Journal of Communication*, *33*(5), pp. 470–503.

2 From Access, Diversity, Equity, and Inclusion to Creative Justice in the U.S. Creative Sector

Theory

In Chapter 1, I described the cultural, historical, political, and social contexts in which the U.S. creative sector exists. I argued that an obsession with power enables and motivates how U.S. society socializes citizens into its cultural, historical, political, and social context, including by casting them into a matrix based on devalued and valued social identities. I also discussed the importance of addressing caste and the discrimination, exclusion, marginalization, oppression, and subjugation that it produces within the creative sector, described my positionality, and closed the chapter with a definition of key terms.

In this chapter, I further define and propose ADEI and *creative justice* as *a* solution to address the enduring wicked problems that caste enables within the U.S. creative sector. I also theorize not only the interlocking relationships that exist between ADEI as practices but also their relationship to achieving *creative justice*. In closing, I argue that as powerbrokers of the creative sector, cultural organizations and the people that they employ should use ADEI as transformation management short-term goals and practices to enable *creative justice*, the long-term goal for which the U.S. creative sector should strive to achieve. By transformation, I mean sustained and profound change to the climate, culture, and people within cultural organizations, and thereby the creative sector.

Globally, creative sectors struggle with how to resolve *creative in*justice. Indeed, cultural workers have struggled to make decisions about how to reconcile funding inequities (Ang & Mar, 2016; Brown, 2014; Gilmore, 1993; Goldbard, 2014; Helicon Collaborative, 2017; Medrano, 2018; Nestruck, 2016; Sidford, 2011); a lack of intentionally engaging with human difference within workforces (cuyler, 2015; Schonfeld et al., 2015; Schonfeld & Sweeney, 2016; Stein, 2000); authentically support cultural organizations about, by, for, and near low casted peoples (cuyler, 2018; Matlon et al., 2014; Rosenstein & Brimer, 2005; Thang Dao-Shah & Faust, 2018; Voss et al., 2016; Yancy Consulting, 2018); and other creative *in*justices that impede peoples' cultural engagement, practices, and values. Although scholars have investigated some of these issues (Bonet & Négrier, 2011; Bodirsky, 2012; cuyler,

DOI: 10.4324/9781003246909-2

2013, 2017a, b, c; cuyler & Hodges, 2015; Jung, 2015; Lähdesmäki, 2012; Leung, 2016; Mirza, 2009; Moss, 2005; Romainville, 2016; Rushton, 2003; Saukkonen & Pyykkönen, 2008; Skot-Hansen, 2002; Taylor, 2017; Yuk, 2016; Zapata-Barreto, 2016), creative *in*justice has received disparate, inconsistent, imbalanced, and unfocused attention in extant literature. Indeed, the literature has also not fully explored or theorized the role that ADEI plays in achieving *creative justice* in the U.S. creative sector. Though, Routledge's series Research in the Creative and Cultural Industries has helped to develop scholarship that aims to address these gaps in the literature (Abfalter & Reitsamer, 2024; Anheier & Markovic, 2024; Eikhof, 2023; Henze & Escribal, 2023; Stein, 2019). In addition, as does Bérubé et al.'s (2024) volume, *Accessibility, Diversity, Equity, and Inclusion in the Cultural Sector: Initiatives and Lessons Learned from Real-Life Cases*.

To frame this chapter, I contemplate the research question: what role does ADEI play in achieving *creative justice* in the U.S. creative sector? Thus, this chapter aims to: (1) make the case for adopting the use of *creative justice* in future discourses about all creative inequities and *in*justices that occur within the creative sector, (2) define ADEI as key short-term goals and practices in and of themselves needed to achieve *creative justice*, and explain how they work together for its manifestation, and (3) re-frame the current discourse on ADEI so that the creative sector sees *creative justice* as the most important long-term goal worthy of pursuit relative to addressing the wicked problem of caste and the impediments that it poses to human flourishing. But what exactly is *creative justice*?

From Social Justice to Creative Justice

As Banks (2017) pointed out, the growth of work in the cultural sector and the creative economy has raised serious questions for social justice. Adams et al. (2007) defined social justice as both a process and a goal:

> Social justice promises full and equal participation of all social groups in a society mutually shaped to meet their needs. Social justice involves social actors who have a sense of their own agency as well as a sense of social responsibility toward and with others, their society, and the broader world in which we live.
>
> (1)

While some cultural workers view culture as a vehicle for rights or political claims (Ross, 1998), or as an instrument for achieving social justice, the claim that culture alone can achieve social justice may overreach given the enormity of inequities and injustices low casted peoples must survive within U.S. society. "Social justice" also encompasses many types of justice claims, including aesthetic, criminal, distributive, educational, economic, epistemic, health, historical, physiological, psychological, and transformational, among others. Yet, social justice's broadness has overwhelmed the creative sector's critical action when seeking to address creative *in*justices. The term's depth has also obscured clarity relative to the creative sector's overall aims and goals regarding it. However, Banks (2017) proposed the term, *creative justice*, to conceptualize what the creative sector should view as its overarching and long-term outcome when seeking to eliminate caste and the creative *in*justices within the creative sector that it produces.

Banks (2017) described *creative justice* as both a descriptive account and a normative aspiration. In defining the term, he provided three "working concepts". The first of which, "objective respect", means to respect cultural objects and practices by evaluating them in terms of their own objective qualities, as well as their subjective apprehension and value. Voss et al. (2016) suggested that this should happen in the creative sector by evaluating affinity cultural organizations with indices and measures uniquely designed to the truth of the ways in which they exist. For example, while some within the creative sector may prescribe what they deem as "good" or "best" management practices, asking the DuSable Museum to behave as the Metropolitan Museum is an unfair and unrealistic expectation, especially given the two museums' age, budget size, histories, origins, and social networks. Nevertheless, when the sector realizes the power of objective respect it can examine how societies allocate and distribute opportunities and rewards, which has implications for who receives the most prestigious cultural education and training, the highest pay, and the best jobs within the creative sector (Banks, 2017).

Banks (2017) identified "parity of participation" as the second concept that contributes to defining *creative justice*. He argued that parity of participation offers a point of commensurability between different types of justice claims. In addition to supporting claims for economic justice such as the re-distribution of wealth in the form of fairer pay, taxation, and social support, it supports the legitimate cultural rights and statuses of all persons. He also suggested that creative sectors adapt the following three foundational principles: (1) advancing social arrangements that allow for the maximum range of people to enter and participate in cultural work, in which they will receive fair treatment, just pay, and reward for their efforts relative to their peers; (2) ensuring that people are not prevented from entering cultural work on the grounds of any unfair cultural discrimination or prejudice, and that they have equal opportunities to participate and develop once they become engaged or employed; and (3) developing the cultural industries as democratic arenas where marginalized groups can advance their own fair representation and secure a more equal share of the public communicative space. He identified blind auditions and selection, recruitment targets and quotas, and fair pay as indicative interventions to achieving parity of participation.

In the U.S., one could synthesize the interventions Banks (2017) described here as affirmative action (cuyler, 2013). However, the U.S. creative sector has not collectively articulated or established the parameters by which it would implement and evaluate these suggested affirmative action policies and practices. In addition, affirmative action remains a highly contested cultural policy in the U.S. due to whom it has most allegedly benefited. Although the perception endures that unqualified people of the global majority, especially Black people have benefited most, Crenshaw (2006) argued that White women have benefited from affirmative action more than any other historically and continuously low casted group in U.S. society.

Finally, Banks (2017) posited reduction of harms as the third and final concept in defining *creative justice*. He maintained that reducing the physical and psychological harms and injuries inflicted by cultural work, based on assessments of objective conditions and their human effects, helps to realize this third working concept. He described some of these harms as aggression, bullying, domination, exploitation, intimidation, overworking, self-exploitation, stress, and/or violence. While Banks (2017) acknowledged that these harms can locate themselves in class, gender, and race-based discrimination and misrecognition, I argue that they also appear in discrimination and biases against those low casted because of their affectional orientation and/or disability status in U.S. society.

Synthesizing Banks' (2017) three working concepts of *creative justice* and re-contextualizing them in U.S. society, I defined *creative justice* as the manifestation of all people living creative and expressive lives on their own terms in 2019. However, high casted peoples, according to the *Matrix of Caste in the U.S.*, already, presumably, live unconstrained creative and expressive lives on their own terms. Thus, in 2021 and 2022, I refined my definition of *creative justice* to the manifestation of all historically discriminated against, marginalized, oppressed, and subjugated peoples living creative and expressive lives on their own terms. Still, after attending the symposium, *Innovating Institutions and Inequities in the Arts* at the Indiana University Center for Cultural Affairs in 2022, my colleague, Dr. Brea Heidelberg, compelled me to consider that the discrimination, marginalization, oppression, othering, subalterning, and subjugation is not only historic but also ongoing (B. Heidelberg, personal communication, June 7, 2022). In addition, Isabelle Wilkerson's *Caste: The Origins of Our Discontent* and the movie about it, *Origin*, compelled me to consider caste as the real wicked problem, and discrimination, exclusion, marginalization, oppression, othering, subalterning, and subjugation as symptoms of it (Wilkerson, 2020). Thus, today, I define *creative justice* as the manifestation of all historically and continuously low casted peoples living creative and expressive lives on their own terms (cuyler, 2023a, 2023b).

ADEI and Creative Justice

Although Banks (2017) developed "creative justice" within the U.K.'s cultural, historical, political, and social context, it has clear implications and resonance for the U.S. In addition, articulating *creative justice* as the long-term goal for the U.S. creative sector to achieve advances the potential of making continued pragmatic progress in addressing the issues that have systemically and systematically impeded low casted peoples' *creative justice*, and thereby their cultural engagement, flourishing, practices, and values within the U.S. creative sector.

To ascertain a deep understanding of the relationships that exist between ADEI and *creative justice*, I also provide clear definitions of ADEI here because in the past cultural workers have borrowed, conflated, de-configured, misunderstood, and misused these terms. In fact, Brown and Brais (2018) found that focus group participants provided wide-ranging definitions of DEI, which made for rich interpretations, but gave little congruence in understanding the terms' actual meanings in practice or theory, and how they could work together to manifest *creative justice*.

Furthermore, one can trace the uses of these terms throughout U.S. history in cultural policies. For example, in the National Foundation on the Arts and Humanities Act of 1965, which established the National Endowment for the Arts (NEA), Congress used the term 'multicultural' to describe the diversity of cultural expressions found within U.S. society (United States of America, 1965). The final passage from the Act stated, "It is vital to democracy to honor and preserve its *multicultural* artistic heritage as well as support new ideas, and therefore it is essential to provide financial assistance to its artists and the organizations that support their work". Over time, the term 'diversity' replaced 'multiculturalism.' More recently, some adopted cultural equity over diversity (Association for Cultural Equity, 2018; Knighton & McCarthy, 2018). However, the creative sector must remember that it cannot choose one short-term goal and practice over the others, and that it must grapple with and manage its work with each of these terms philosophically, pragmatically, realistically, theoretically, and strategically as they do not have the same meaning or serve the same purposes. To otherwise do so is reductionist and crippling to making meaningful progress on addressing enduring systemic creative *in*justice within the creative sector (Cuyler, 2023a).

The confusion and lack of understanding of ADEI may also explain why some low casted cultural workers' frustrations with the language used to describe their lived experiences justify their belief that the creative sector's interest in and willingness to address creative *in*justices cycles through a ten-year period when the next 'fad' occurs without the creative sector making any meaningful progress on eliminating creative *in*justice. Still, again, ADEI are different short-term goals and practices, each requiring their own unique strategy to address specific low casted groups (cuyler, 2017a; cuyler, 2017b; cuyler, 2017c; cuyler, 2018; cuyler, 2019; cuyler, 2021; cuyler, 2022; DeVos Institute of Arts Management, 2015), and each plays a significant role in achieving seismic and transformational sectoral wide *creative justice*.

Access

I define access as the removal of all barriers to participation in the creative sector. I define participation broadly to include early exposure to arts education to adult arts education, singing in a church choir, watching performances on YouTube, and in-person attendance, among other types of participation. To achieve access, the creative sector must interrogate all the barriers and hurdles low casted peoples face when attempting to engage in culture. Some of these barriers might include price, time, transportation, or even emotional and psychological barriers such as the fear of not belonging. Most importantly, the creative sector must eliminate all barriers and hurdles to equal participation by creating multiple entry points to all types of cultural engagement. A good question to ask when thinking about access is: are all the doors to the ways in which humans can engage with the cultural organization or the creative sector open to all people, and specifically, all low casted peoples? If the answer is no, then the sector and its power brokers must take all opportunities to do so seriously as their nonprofit status requires it.

Diversity

Scholars have defined diversity in many ways. In defining diversity, Loden (1995) and my previous definition (cuyler, 2013) are useful for examining two different approaches to similar meanings. Loden (1995) viewed diversity as human differences more likely to lead to a cultural clash when humans devalue, ignore, or misunderstand them. I (2013) defined diversity as the acceptance, acknowledgment, and proactive use of the fact of human differences in practice. However, my thinking has evolved. Today, I amend my definition of diversity to a qualitative and/or quantitative assessment of the intentional engagement of human difference, which one could deem as several demographic and ideological characteristics and qualities. Pursuing representation across the full spectrum of human differences is important because those who experience creative *in*justice have systemically and systematically had their cultural engagement, flourishing, practices, and values constrained by societal reinforcing of internalized inferiority through the *Matrix of Caste in U.S. society*.

Equity

Although Banks (2017) made a case for using both equality and equity, some within the U.S. creative sector use these terms interchangeably even though they are not the same. In equality, on day one, everyone receives the same exact opportunity to flourish and achieve success. Equity, however, goes further than equality by assessing what intervention(s) one truly needs to succeed and provides it especially because of long-suffered inequality. While Knighton and McCarthy (2018) rightly criticize the term 'cultural equity' as the new place holder for 'multiculturalism' and 'diversity', ethnomusicologist, Dr. Alan Lomax, advocated for cultural equity in 1972 when his studies revealed that mass communications and centralized education systems crushed local languages and expressive traditions (Association of Cultural Equity, 2018).

Cultural equity, then, is the preservation of all cultural practices and traditions in all arts disciplines through the equitable distribution of financial resources. All artistic and cultural products hold the same value and should receive appropriate resources to ensure their successful competition in the market and dissemination to all people. Indeed, opera and gospel hold equal importance, as well as African dance and ballet, or Baroque and Pop art. Allocating much of the creative sector's philanthropic industrial complex to legacy cultural organizations whose budgets trend above $5 million and primarily serve white audiences and visitors (Helicon Collaborative, 2017) sends a clear message that only Western European cultural traditions are deserving and worthy of preservation, and that only white people are worthy of aesthetic representation. When thinking about cultural equity, the U.S. creative sector must consider what it loses, in terms of creative assets, when it ostracizes the cultural practices, traditions, and values of people from historically and continuously low casted populations. Thus, I define equity as fairness in addressing historic, continuous, and long-suffered inequality by low casted groups.

Inclusion

As the counterweight to exclusion, inclusion means to create community through a sense of belonging. To practice inclusion effectively, the U.S. creative sector needs to do a great deal of critical listening to become more inclusive of low casted peoples. The result of critical listening could mean fixing broken systems of support or conceptualizing and envisioning new and more equitable systems in which all cultural organizations, practices, traditions, and values can co-exist harmoniously. Furthermore, Taylor (2017) defined inclusion as an organizational environment where everyone can reach his or her full potential. In pursuing inclusion, the creative sector should think seriously about the loss of talent that it, cultural organizations, and their networks suffer when low casted peoples do not feel that they can reach their full potential. This is key when contextualizing cultural organizations' roles in perpetuating White supremacy in a society that for years excluded the global majority, LGBTQ+ people, poor people, people with disabilities, women and 'othered' gender identities from fully participating in and actualizing their *creative justice* through cultural engagement and cultural rights.

As short-term goals and practices in and of themselves, ADEI, then, enables achieving *creative justice*. When the creative sector operationalizes ADEI with authenticity and intentionality, it leads to *creative justice*, which is the long-term goal for which the creative sector should strive. In addition, ADEI has a great deal of synergy with Banks' (2017) "working concepts" used to define *creative justice*. For example, access and parity of participation mirror each other because they aim to bolster the cultural engagement of all low casted peoples. Equity, cultural or otherwise, has resonance with object respect as the need to evaluate cultural objects on their own objective qualities, as well as their subjective apprehension and value. The reduction of harms aligns with inclusion, given that critical listening would make it possible for the creative sector to become more inclusive and rid itself of aggression, bullying, domination, exploitation, intimidation, overworking, self-exploitation, stress, or violence. While it appears to lack a parallel, diversity serves as the leitmotif that implicitly occurs throughout the definition of all these goals and practices.

Figure 2.1 provides a visual representation of the relationships between ADEI and *creative justice*. Maintaining the ideal that the creative sector should prioritize achieving *creative justice* as its primary long-term goal, I situate *creative justice* at the center of the model arguing that ADEI remains in constant motion orbiting around and linked to *creative justice*. If the U.S. creative sector truly aspires to make progress toward replacing systemic creative *in*justice produced by caste with systemic *creative justice*, it must develop specific and targeted strategies related to the transformation leadership and management short-term goals and practices of ADEI. The creative sector will need to make the strategies specific, but wide-reaching because creative *in*justice remains deeply imbedded in systems that have been normalized throughout the development and evolution of the creative sector. The equation I theorize here, then, is (A)ccess+(D)iversity+(E)quity+(I)nclusion = Creative Justice (CJ).

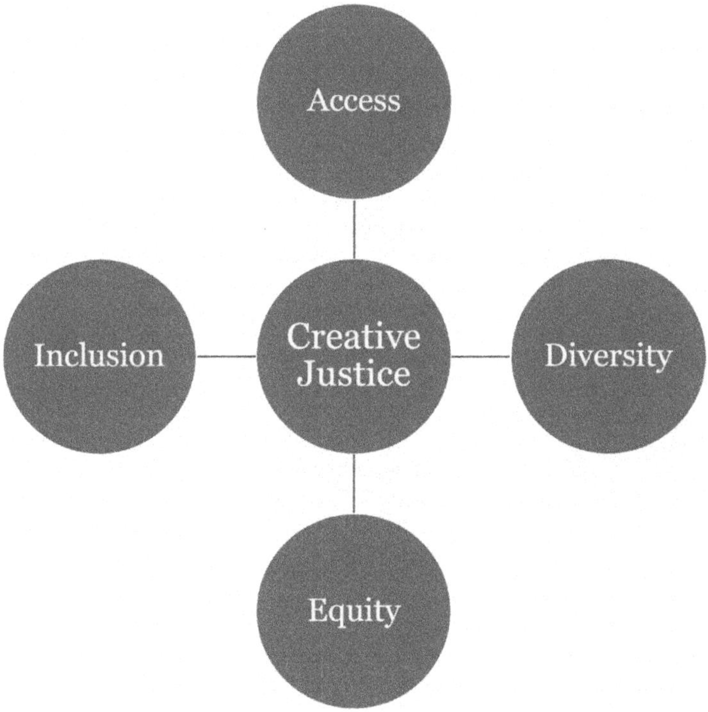

Figure 2.1 The Creative Justice Conceptual and Theoretical Framework.

Conclusion

In closing, I want to remind readers that in 1983, Audre Lorde said, "There is no hierarchy of oppressions". If true, then the creative sector would benefit from viewing all forms of caste as equally worthy of elimination. In the first part of this chapter, I explored the research question: What role does ADEI play in achieving *creative justice* in the U.S. creative sector? I also advocated for adopting the use of the term *creative justice* in future discourses as a more exact and precise way to frame progress and goals for the creative sector to pursue in the U.S. I also defined ADEI as key short-term goals and practices needed to enable the transformation leadership and management needed to achieve *creative justice* in the U.S. creative sector. I also explained how they work together for its manifestation.

In Chapter 3, I will operationalize the theory of *creative justice* by introducing the *Creative Justice Procedural Model* which theorizes the process by which the creative sector and its power brokers (cultural organizations and the people in which they employ) can practically use ADEI to manifest *creative justice*. I also pose five questions to help readers interrogate their own practices and improve their strategies for achieving *creative justice* **with** low casted peoples.

References

Abfalter, D., & Reitsamer, R. (2024). *Music as Labour: Inequalities and Activism in the Past and Present*. Routledge.

Adams, M., Bell, L. A., & Griffin, P. (2007). *Teaching for Diversity and Social Justice*, 2nd Ed. New York, NY: Routledge.

Ang, I., & Mar, P. (2016). Australia's Arts Community Has a Big Diversity Problem – That's Our Loss. https://theconversation.com/australias-arts-community-has-a-big-diversity-problem-thats-our-loss-52686

Anheier, H., & Markovic, D. (2024). *Gender Equality and the Cultural Economy: Comparative Perspectives*. Routledge.

Association for Cultural Equity. (2018). Cultural Equity. http://culturalequity.org/ace/cultural-equity

Banks, M. (2017). *Creative Justice: Cultural Industries, Work, and Inequality*. London: Rowman & Littlefield International.

Bérubé, J., Dioh, M. L., & cuyler, a. c. (2024). *Accessibility, Diversity, Equity, and Inclusion in the Cultural Sector: Initiative and Lessons Learned from Real-Life Cases*. Emerald Publishing.

Bodirsky, K. (2012). Culture for Competitiveness: Valuing Diversity in EU-Europe and the 'Creative City' of Berlin. *International Journal of Cultural Policy*, *18*(4), pp. 455–473.

Bonet, L., & Négrier, E. (2011). The End(s) of National Cultures? Cultural Policy in the Face of Diversity. *International Journal of Cultural Policy*, *17*(5), pp. 574–589.

Brown, M. (2014, December 7). Arts in England Told to Make Progress With Diversity or Have Funding Axed. *The Guardian*. http://theguardian.com/uk-news/2014/dec/08/arts-council-england-make-progress-diversity-funding-axed-bazalgette

Brown, M. T., & Brais, H. (2018). *Examining Cultural Equity in the Arts*. https://static1.squarespace.com/static/582a427250161e43d93cff2/t/5a6bcf67652dea6889e1c5ae/1517014890763/CEG+COMMUNITY+REPORT+FINAL.p

Crenshaw, K. (2006). Framing Affirmative Action. *Michigan Law Review First Impressions*, *105*, pp. 123–133.

cuyler, a. c. (2013). Affirmative Action and Diversity: Implications for Arts Management. *Journal of Arts Management, Law, and Society*, *43*(2), pp. 1–15.

cuyler, a. c. (2015). An Exploratory Study of Demographic Diversity in the Arts Management Workforce. *GIA Reader*, *26*(3), pp. 1–4.

cuyler, a. c. (2017a). The Effects of Diversity on U.S. Arts Managers' Managerial Level and Salary. *American Journal of Arts Management*, *5*(1), pp. 1–10.

cuyler, a. c. (2017b). A Survey of Arts Management Educators' Teaching on Diversity Issues. *Journal of Arts Management, Law, and Society*, *47*(3), pp. 1–10.

cuyler, a. c. (2017c). U.S. Executive Arts Managers: A Descriptive Analysis of Their Demographic Diversity, Salary & Benefits, and Job Satisfaction. *Cultural Management: Science and Education*, *1*(2), pp. 1–8.

cuyler, a. c. (2018). The Efficacy of Using Service Learning to Teach about Social Justice Issues in the U.S. Cultural Sector. *International Journal of Social, Political, and Community Agendas in the Arts*, *13*(4), pp. 19–28.

cuyler, a. c. (2019). The Role of Foundations in Achieving Creative Justice in the U.S. Cultural Sector. *Grantmakers In the Arts Reader*, *30*(1), p. 6.

cuyler, a. c. (2021). Diversity, Equity, and Inclusion (DEI) Statements in the U.S. Creative Sector: Progress, or More Bullshit? *Cultural Management: Science and Education*, *5*(2), p. 16.

cuyler, a. c. (2022). Moving Beyond @Operaisracist: Exploring Blacktivism as a Pathway to Antiracism and Creative Justice in Opera. In D. Abfalter & R. Reitsamer (Eds.), *Music as Labour: Inequalities and Activism in the Past and Present* (pp. 204–218). Routledge.

cuyler, a. c. (2023a). Review of the Books Creative Justice: Cultural Industries, Work, and Inequality and Race and the Cultural Industries. *International Journal of Cultural Policy*, *29*(3), pp. 395–399.

cuyler, a. c. (2023b). Casualties of Exclusionary Cultural Policies: Exploring the Paradox of Black American Cultural Engagement. *Journal for Cultural Research*, *27*(1), pp. 23–37.

cuyler, a. c., & Hodges, A. (2015). From the Student Side of the Ivory Tower: An Empirical Study of Student Expectations of Internships in Arts and Cultural Management. *International Journal of Arts Management*, *17*(3), pp. 68–79.

DeVos Institute of Arts Management. (2015). Diversity in the Arts: The Past, Present, and Future of African American and Latino Museums, Dance Companies, and Theatre Companies. http://devosinstitute.umd.edu/What-We-Do/News-and-Announcements/Announcements/Announcements/Diversity%20in%20the%20Arts%20paper

Eikhof, D. (2023). *Diversity and Inclusion: Are We There Yet? Target Setting in the Screen Industries*. Routledge.

Gilmore, S. (1993). Minorities and Distributional Equity at the National Endowment for the Arts. *Journal of Arts Management, Law, and Society*, *23*(2), pp. 137–173.

Goldbard, A. (2014). Cultural Equity: An Opera in Three Acts. http://stirjournal.com/2014/09/08/cultural-equity-an-opera-in-three-acts/

Helicon Collaborative. (2017). Not Just Money: Equity Issues in Cultural Philanthropy. http://notjustmoney.us/

Henze, R., & Escribal, F. (2023). *Cultural Management and Policy in Latin America*. Routledge.

Jung, Y. (2015). Diversity Matters: Theoretical Understanding of and Suggestions for the Current Fundraising Practices of Nonprofit Art Museums. *Journal of Arts Management, Law, and Society*, *45*(4), pp. 255–268.

Knighton, M., & McCarthy, K. (2018). Beyond Equity as a Trend, Toward Real Change. http://ddcf.org/what-were-learning/beyond-equity-as-a-trend-toward-real-change/

Lähdesmäki, T. (2012). Rhetoric of Unity and Cultural Diversity in the Making of European Cultural Identity. *International Journal of Cultural Policy*, *18*(1), pp. 59–75.

Leung, L. (2016). The Creative Other: Marginalization of and from the Creative Industries. *Journal of Arts Management, Law, and Society*, *46*(4), pp. 200–211.

Loden, M. (1995). *Implementing Diversity*. New York, NY: McGraw-Hill Education.

Lorde, A. (1983). There Is No Hierarchy of Oppressions. *Interracial Books for Children Bulletin*, *14*(3–4), p. 9.

Matlon, M., Van Haastrecht, I., & Mengüç, K. (2014). Figuring the Plural: Needs and Supports of Canadian and US Ethnocultural Arts Organizations. https://arts.gov/sites/default/files/Research-Art-Works-ArtChicago-rev.pdf

Medrano, A. (2018). A Call to Collaborate: Continued Inequity in Funding Houston LatinX Arts Organizations 2010–2015. https://app.box.com/s/aplzciflkv5pr0xp2nvnly0y4am0cpnu

Mirza, M. (2009). Aims and Contradictions of Cultural Diversity Policies in the Arts: A Case Study of the Rich Mix Centre in East London. *International Journal of Cultural Policy*, *15*(1), pp. 53–69.

Moss, L. (2005). Biculturalism and Cultural Diversity. *International Journal of Cultural Policy*, *11*(2), pp. 187–197.

Nestruck, K. (2016). Canada Council's Diversity Focus Brings New Opportunities, Challenges. https://theglobeandmail.com/arts/theatre-and-performance/canada-councils-diversity-focus-brings-new-opportunities-challenges/article28212718/

Rainbow Resource Center. (2012). Heterosexism. https://rainbowresourcecentre.org/files/12-11-Heterosexism.pdf

Romainville, C. (2016). Cultural Diversity as a Multilevel and Multifaceted Legal Notion Operating in the Law on Cultural Policies. *International Journal of Cultural Policy*, *22*(2), pp. 273–290.

Rosenstein, C., & Brimer, A. (2005). Nonprofit Ethnic, Cultural, and Folk Organizations: Baseline Data from the National Center for Charitable Statistics. *Journal of Arts Management, Law, and Society*, *35*(3), pp. 189–203.

Ross, A. (1998). *Real Love: In Pursuit of Cultural Justice*. London: Routledge.

Rushton, M. (2003). Cultural Diversity and Public Funding of the Arts: A View from Cultural Economics. *Journal of Arts Management, Law, and Society*, *33*(2), pp. 85–97.

Saukkonen, P., & Pyykkönen, M. (2008). Cultural Policy and Cultural Diversity in Finland. *International Journal of Cultural Policy*, *14*(1), pp. 49–63.

Schonfeld, R., & Sweeney, L. (2016). Diversity in New York City Department of Cultural Affairs Community. http://sr.ithaka.org/publications/diversity-in-the-new-york-city-department-of-cultural-affairs-community/

Schonfeld, R., Westermann, M., & Sweeney, L. (2015). The Andrew W. Mellon Foundation Art Museum Staff Demographic Survey. https://mellon.org/media/filer_public/ba/99/ba99e53a-48d5-4038-80e1-66f9ba1c020e/awmf_museum_diversity_report_aamd_7-28-15.pdf

Sidford, H. (2011). Fusing Arts, Culture and Social Change. https://ncrp.org/publication/fusing-arts-culture-social-change

Skot-Hansen, D. (2002). Danish Cultural Policy –From Monoculture Towards Cultural Diversity. *International Journal of Cultural Policy*, *8*(2), pp. 197–210.

Stein, T. (2000). Creating Opportunities for People of Color in Performing Arts Management. *Journal of Arts Management, Law, and Society*, *29*(4), pp. 304–318.

Stein, T. (2019). *Racial and Ethnic Diversity in the Performing Arts Workforce*. Routledge.

Taylor, C. (2017). From Systemic Exclusion to Systemic Inclusion: A Critical Look at Museums. *Journal of Art Museum Education*, *42*(2), pp. 155–162.

Thang Dao-Shah, A., & Faust, K. (2018). Mapping Small Arts & Culture Organizations of Color in Oakland. http://mapartscultureoakland.org/wp-content/uploads/Mapping_Oakland_061918.pdf

United States of America. (1965). National Foundation on the Arts and the Humanities Act of 1965. https://neh.gov/about/history/national-foundation-arts-and-humanities-act-1965-pl-89-209

Voss, Z., Voss, G., Louie, A., Drew, Z., & Teyolia, M. (2016). National Center for Arts Research: Does "Strong and Effective" Look Different for Culturally Specific Arts Organizations? http://smu.edu/~/media/Site/Meadows/NCAR/NCARWhitePaper01-12

Wilkerson, I. (2020). *Cast: The Origins of Our Discontent*. Random House.

Yancy Consulting. (2018). What Are the Paradigm Shifts Necessary for the Arts Sector to Nurture More Sustainable THRIVING Institutions of Color? http://ddcf.org/globalassets/news-and-publications/2018-news-and-publications/final-yancey-consultings-alaana-thrivability-report-january-2018.pdf

Yuk, J. (2016). Interrogating the Uses of Culture in the Politics of Diversity: A Case from South Korea. *International Journal of Cultural Policy*, *22*(4), pp. 516–533.

Zapata-Barrero, R. (2016). Diversity and Cultural Policy: Cultural Citizenship as a Tool for Inclusion. *International Journal of Cultural Policy*, *22*(4), pp. 534–552.

3 The Creative Justice Procedural Model

Practice

The incomparable opera singer, Leontyne Price, said,

> All token Blacks have the same experience. I have been pointed at as a solution to things that have not yet begun to be solved, because pointing at us token Blacks eases consciences of millions, and this is dreadfully wrong.
>
> (Illinois Commission on the Status of Women, 1985, p. 115)

As readers move into operationalizing ADEI toward *creative justice*, I discourage the practice of tokenization through representation. Representation alone is not the work, but simply a start to the work. As an example, by most measures, women are well-represented across multiple positionalities within U.S. orchestras, except for as conductors and music directors (cuyler et al., 2023). However, women continue to experience an anti-woman culture that penalizes them for their representation via pay inequities, for example, at the Boston Symphony Orchestra (Tsioulcas, 2019) and sexual assault at the New York Philharmonic (Sussman, 2024). The creative sector's work, then, is to build a 'culture of care' that enables *creative justice* and flourishing **with** all low casted peoples.

In Chapter 1, I described the cultural, historical, political, and social contexts in which the U.S. creative sector exists. I argued that an obsession with power motivates how the U.S. creative sector socializes people to its context, including by casting them into a matrix based on devalued and valued social identities. I also discussed the importance of addressing caste and the discrimination, exclusion, marginalization, oppression, othering, subalterning, and subjugation that it produces within the creative sector. I described my positionality and closed the chapter by defining key terms. In Chapter 2, I further defined and proposed ADEI as short-term goals and practices in pursuit of *creative justice* as *a* solution to address the enduring wicked problem of caste within the U.S. creative sector. I also theorized the relationships that exist between ADEI as practices, and their roles in manifesting *creative justice*. In closing, I argued that ADEI are the short-term goals and practices that

DOI: 10.4324/9781003246909-3

the creative sector should use to achieve *creative justice*, the long-term goal, which I defined as the manifestation of all historically and continuously low caste peoples living creative and expressive lives on their own terms.

In this chapter, I describe the motivations for practicing ADEI in service to achieving *creative justice*. I also operationalize the theory of *creative justice* discussed in Chapter 2 by introducing the Creative Justice Procedural Model, which describes the process by which ADEI leads to *creative justice*. To do this, I pose five reflective prompts as questions designed to help the creative sector and its power brokers plan and improve their practice of ADEI and strategies toward achieving *creative justice*. These questions include: (1) to what extent have you and your cultural organization removed barriers to participation **with** historically and continuously low casted peoples? (2) to what extent are historically and continuously low casted peoples engaged in roles throughout and within your cultural organization and personal network? (3) to what extent have you and your cultural organization addressed historic, continuous, and long-suffered inequality **with** historically and continuously low casted peoples through policies and practices? (4) to what extent have you and your cultural organization created a culture of belonging **with** historically and continuously low casted peoples? (5) what are the implications for the creative sector if you and your cultural organization do not address caste that results in creative *in*justices for historically and continuously low casted peoples? Readers will note that I bolded the word '**with**' to remind high casted peoples to avoid saviorism in working to transform cultural organizations toward *creative justice*. Too often, when the creative sector, and the cultural organizations that comprise it, pursue *creative justice* 'at,' 'for,' or 'to' instead of **with** low casted peoples, it does not go as well as low caste people would like. **With** explicitly requires that high and low casted peoples must work together to achieve *creative justice* within the creative sector.

Furthermore, as an ADEI consultant who partners with and coach cultural organizations on maximizing their performance and community relevance through ADEI, I have worked closely with choruses, museums, opera companies, orchestras, youth cultural organizations, and professional trade associations within the creative sector. Cultural organizations and the people that they employ are the creative sector's most valuable sentinels of *creative justice*. Often when working with my clients, I find them eager to move on to doing 'the work'. But the work remains complicated and constrained by their actual readiness to do 'the work'. Usually, this includes a discussion of U.S. history and how the creative sector came to need to practice ADEI. But also, a discussion of the ten myths and misunderstandings about ADEI (cuyler, 2023), which include:

1. We welcome everyone, and do not need to do ADEI.
2. We want to do ADEI, but we do not know where to begin and we do not want to make a mistake.

3. We want to do ADEI, but we do not want to change.
4. We do not need to budget for ADEI because it is not worth the money.
5. ADEI and artistic excellence are not complimentary. We would have to lower our standards to pursue ADEI.
6. ADEI does not benefit us.
7. We cannot use ADEI to diversify our board because we do not know any Black, Indigenous, or People of Color (BIPOC).
8. ADEI is only about ethnicity, gender, and/or race.
9. ADEI is divisive and political.
10. "I am privileged by my ability, affectional orientation, age, class, gender, political party affiliation, race, and/or religion. When it comes to ADEI, I need to just keep my mouth shut and listen".

I always recommend that my clients use an evidence-based approach to doing "the work" of ADEI because, epistemologically, it situates their practice in knowing and critically examining themselves, which optimizes their use of ADEI to lead and manage organizational transformation that will increase their chances of achieving *creative justice*. After coaching cultural organizations on how to respond to the active and passive resistance that may materialize through the ten myths and misunderstandings about ADEI, I facilitate information gathering through a climate, culture, and people survey and/or focus groups. Using an information-gathering approach to leading and managing organizational transformation remains critical to the success of cultural organizations' ADEI work. I also remind cultural organizations of the four motivations for why they should practice ADEI to achieve *creative justice*.

First, cultural organizations should practice ADEI to achieve *creative justice* because of its explicit ethical and moral imperative. Simply put, it is the right thing to do. In a society that some humans designed to exist as unequal; course correcting so that everyone has equal access to the opportunity to develop their full potential and flourish greatly benefits individuals and society. It is also critical for social cohesion. No one should have their potential constrained by their ability, affectional orientation, age, class, gender, political party affiliation, race, religion, astrological sign, or any other identity that makes humans beautifully different. All people deserve the opportunity to succeed. Society, and by extension, the creative sector, should explicitly ensure and protect this sacred right.

Second, cultural organizations should practice ADEI to achieve *creative justice* because of their mission imperative to educate communities. However, time (47%), costs (38%), difficult to get to (37%), no one to go with (22%), did not want to go to the location (9%), and lack of interest in the programs (7%) (National Endowment for the Arts, 2015) constrain peoples' *creative justice*. While pursuing their missions, cultural organizations must remain curious about learning the ways to address these barriers. In addition, as they pursue their missions to educate communities, cultural organizations also have a social responsibility to

> (1) actively participate in the liberation of the culturally disenfranchised, (2) support and pursue opportunities for decentralized cultural policy, (3) encourage broad based representative research and decision-making and pluralistic distribution mechanisms for financing cultural activities, (4) dedicate a significant portion of the work week studying the system in order to sharpen understanding of it, (5) publicly urge the creation and periodic updates of a comprehensive and sensitive community cultural assessment, (6) enable and serve as accomplices to and for activism where past exclusionary social patterns have established cultural inequities, and (7) remain aware of monopolies in the creative sector and develop compensatory responses to barriers to entry.
>
> (cuyler, 2019; Gilmore, 1993; Helicon Collaborative, 2017; Keller, 1989; Sidford, 2011)

Doing so helps them to fulfill the implicit promise of *creative justice* espoused and envisioned in the National Foundation on the Arts and Humanities Act of 1965 (National Endowment for the Humanities, 1965).

Third, cultural organizations should practice ADEI to achieve *creative justice* because of their structural imperative. As nonprofit organizations with 501(c) 3 statuses, cultural organizations must remain equally accessible to all people, including those who have experienced historic, continuous, and long-suffered low caste. The tax status granted to cultural organizations by the U.S. Internal Revenue Service (IRS) also suggests that the *public* owns nonprofit cultural organizations. Because the full slate of social identity groups in the U.S. comprises the public and communities, the enterprise of public ownership, ethically, legally, morally, practically, and theoretically excludes no one. Well-aligned with their missions, as nonprofits owned by the public, achieving *creative justice* protects cultural organizations from losing their 501(c)3 tax status. Anderson (2016) and Lowery (2023) defined "Whitelash" as a phenomenon of White racial violence embedded in U.S. society not just in the last few election cycles, but since the nation's founding (Kaplan, 2023). This Whitelash has unleashed a torrent of legal attacks on ADEI by a well-funded network of conservative activists occurring in U.S. society in response to the 2020 summer of racial discontent.

People of the global majority and other historically and continuously low casted peoples who have long, and quietly endured their status in society will begin fighting back by calling into question the nonprofit tax status of cultural organizations who blatantly and fragrantly engage in caste and the discrimination, exclusion, marginalization, oppression, othering, subalterning, and subjugation that it produces. Achieving *creative justice* will proactively protect cultural organizations from this impending pendulum swing if they clearly show that their mission, goals, and practices for achieving it aligns with their structural imperative and manifesting *creative justice*. As goals and practices in and of themselves, ADEI remain essential to ensuring that all people within communities have equal opportunities to consume, engage in, create, experience, and express culture.

Fourth, cultural organizations should practice ADEI to achieve *creative justice* because of the economic imperative. I placed the economic motivation last purposely because though this book has implications for the for-profit creative sector, too, in this book, I speak specifically to the nonprofit creative sector, which should prioritize doing good in society over generating profits, as implicit in their legal entity's structure. Fortunately, nonprofit cultural organizations do not have to choose between doing good and earning revenue. They can, indeed, do both. As stated in Chapter 2, Becker (1971) theorized that "discrimination in the marketplace by any group reduces the discriminator's income as well as those discriminated against because of their social identities" in *The Economics of Discrimination*. His theory revealed the irrationality of caste in an alleged capitalist society. If it is true that historically and continuously low casted peoples have buying power in U.S. society, then adopting an anti-caste ethos and practice remains good for business. Indeed, true capitalists understand that the most profitable corporations are also the least biased (Miller & Katz, 2024). But, by what process might the creative sector achieve *creative justice*?

Creative Justice Procedural Model

The U.S. creative sector can achieve *creative justice* by practicing ADEI systematically, step by step to lead and manage organizational transformation. To support cultural organizations in their process, I propose the Creative Justice Procedural Model. Considering the four short-term goals and practices that comprise ADEI as steps along a stairwell, access is the first step in the process toward *creative justice* and the foundational building block on which cultural organizations' *creative justice* strategy depends. Readers will recall that in Chapters 1 and 2, I defined access as the removal of all barriers to participation. Access enables diversity, which is the second step. I also defined diversity as a qualitative and/or quantitative assessment of the intentional engagement of human differences.

After access and diversity, cultural organizations can proceed to the third step of equity. I defined equity as fairness in addressing historic, continuous, and long-suffered inequality. Cultural organizations proceed to the fourth step, inclusion, after assessing the failures and successes of their access, diversity, and equity short-term goals and practices. I defined inclusion as belonging, the antithesis of exclusion. Inclusion is likely the most difficult of these four short-term goals and practices because it depends on how everyone

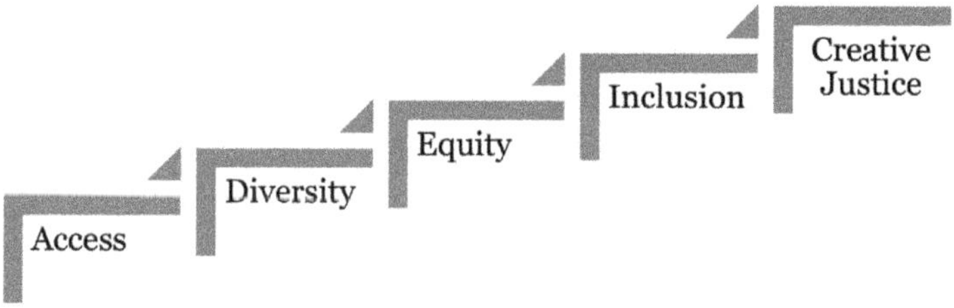

Figure 3.1 The Creative Justice Procedural Model.

the cultural organization engages with personally experiences it across multiple identities, positionalities, and roles. Figure 3.1 depicts that *creative justice* rest at the top of the stairwell after cultural organizations have effectively and systematically practiced ADEI to ascertain it for every group of low casted peoples.

Readers should keep in mind that depending on the low casted group they will not require the same intentionality of all the practices. For example, LGB+ peoples and women remain overrepresented in the creative sector in comparison to their representation in U.S. society. The creative sector and cultural organizations will need to focus on equity and inclusion when it comes to addressing *creative justice* for these low casted groups. Conversely, cultural organizations will have to start with access and work systematically through inclusion to address creative *in*justice experienced by people with disabilities and of the global majority because their representation in the creative sector lags their representation in U.S. society (cuyler, 2023). Furthermore, users of the model should assess their progress incrementally as they move through each step. If cultural organizations observe a lack of diversity or intentional engagement with a specific low casted group, this should indicate the need to take a step back to access to continue removing barriers to participation for the specific identified low casted group. Lastly, cultural organizations can use this thinking at any step along the Creative Justice Procedural Model so that the process constantly cycles through refining itself to ensure desired outcomes and success.

ADEI remains the building blocks of a truly meritocratic society and creative sector, which also enables excellence. No longer can the creative sector afford to abuse, exclude, and mistreat low casted peoples in the name of beauty. In fact, when I consume and experience cultural products, I would like to know, how humanely did cultural organizations produce the work? How much care, compassion, and concern did people experience on their way to creating and making culture? Though some believe differently, identity-based human suffering is not a necessary ingredient of artistic excellence and artistic merit. Still, relative to leading and managing organizational transformation, Fogg (2024) offered a useful formula, B=MAP. For cultural organizations to adopt ADEI as a framework for goal setting and strategy, their motivation (M), ability (A), and a prompt (P) must converge (Brown, 2024). To deepen cultural organizations' practice of using ADEI to envision, plan, explore, and evaluate their organizational transformation toward *creative justice* with care, creativity, innovation, and intentionality, I offer the ADEI assessment instrument that follows based on the *Matrix of Caste in the U.S.* that I presented in Chapter 1.

ADEI Assessment Instrument

Based on a scale from 1 to 3, with 1 as the least and 3 as the greatest, choose the number that best represents the cultural organization's engagement with the specific low casted peoples below as artists, audience members, board members, donors/funders, partners, staff, vendors, and/or volunteers. Use the last section to reflect on individual personal networks. I encourage cultural organizations to complete this assessment collaboratively with the board and staff to gain a deeper understanding of how the board and staff may view the organization differently based on their positionalities within the organization, which will likely offer indicators of the organization's climate and culture. I also encourage employees to conduct the assessment of their personal networks individually. Cultural workers have incredible human capital that could help to bolster the social capital and impact of the cultural organizations that employ them. Once completed, the assessment should help cultural organizations and their employees envision, plan, explore, and evaluate their organizational transformation goals toward *creative justice* (Table 3.1).

Reflective Prompts

1. Based on your assessments, with which low casted peoples have you and/or your cultural organization most often engaged with, and why?
2. With which low casted peoples have you and/or your cultural organization least often engaged with, and why?
3. Would the low casted peoples in your community agree with your assessment, and why?
4. What specific, measurable, achievable, relevant, and time bound (SMART) goals can you articulate to help you envision, plan, explore, and evaluate your strategy to achieve *creative justice* for each group of low casted peoples in your cultural organization and personal network?

In this chapter, I introduced the Creative Justice Procedural Model which describes how ADEI leads to *creative justice*. I proposed Fogg's (2024) formula for behavioral change, B=MAP, to support cultural organizations' understanding of the components that enable organizational transformation

Table 3.1 ADEI Assessment Instrument

Roles & Low Casted Peoples	Access	Diversity	Equity	Inclusion
	–	–	–	-
	To what extent have you and your cultural organization removed barriers to participation **with** historically and continuously low casted peoples in the roles listed below?	To what extent do you intentionally engage historically and continuously low casted peoples in the roles listed below?	To what extent have you and your cultural organization addressed long suffered historic, continuous, and long suffered unfairness **with** historically and continuously low casted peoples through policies and practices in the role listed below?	To what extent have you and your cultural organization created a culture of belonging **with** historically and continuously low casted peoples in the roles below?
As Artists (Actors, Composers, Conductors, Curators, Directors, Musicians, Singers, Soloists, Stage Managers, etc.)				
1. African/Black American				
2. Agnostic				
3. Asexual				
4. Asian American				
5. Atheist				
6. Bi-sexual				
7. Gay				
8. Green Party				
9. Hindu				

(*Continued*)

Table 3.1 (Continued)

10. Hispanic/Latin American
11. Immigrant
12. Independent
13. Indigenous American
14. Jewish
15. Lesbian
16. Libertarian
17. Middle Eastern & North African American
18. Multi-racial American
19. Muslim
20. Non-affiliate
21. Nonbinary
22. Queer
23. People w/Disabilities
24. People younger than 40.
25. People 40+
26. People who live in rural towns.
27. Poor
28. Same Gender Loving
29. Santerían
30. Trans men
31. Trans women
32. Wiccan

(*Continued*)

Table 3.1 (Continued)

As Audiences Members
*Repeat above list of low casted peoples.
As Board Members
*Repeat above list of low casted peoples.
As Donors/Funders
*Repeat above list of low casted peoples.
As Partners
*Repeat above list of low casted peoples.
As Staff
*Repeat above list of low casted peoples.
As Vendors
*Repeat above list of low casted peoples.
As Volunteers
*Repeat above list of low casted peoples.
Your Personal Network
*Repeat above list of low casted peoples.

toward *creative justice*. I described the motivations for practicing ADEI to achieve *creative justice*. Lastly, I presented the ADEI assessment instrument to empower cultural organizations in their ability to practically lead and manage organizational transformation toward *creative justice*, including reflective prompts to help them plan their goals and practice of ADEI for achieving *creative justice*.

The ADEI assessment instrument does not portend comprehensiveness. It is a tool to help cultural organizations think systematically about the groups of low casted peoples that exist in their communities, and how they might engage low casted groups explicitly and intentionally in the range of roles that exist within the organization. In Chapter 4, I will survey the creative sector for examples of how cultural organizations currently practice ADEI, which may lead the creative sector to achieve *creative justice*.

References

Anderson, C. (2016). *White Rage: The Unspoken Truth of Our Racial Divide*. Bloomsbury.

Becker, G. (1971). *The Economics of Discrimination*, 2nd Ed. University of Chicago Press.

Brown, G. (2024, March 1). Why Quitting Can Be a Superpower That Helps Your Mental Health. *The Washington Post*. https://washingtonpost.com/wellness/2024/03/01/quitting-smart-strategies-benefits/?utm_campaign=wp_post_most&utm_medium=email&utm_source=newsletter&wpisrc=nl_most&carta-url=https%3A%2F%2Fs2.washingtonpost.com%2Fcar-ln-tr%2F3cecbad%2F65e208213daa071b49b6974d%2F610045b5ade4e20d1441668b%2F23%2F53%2F65e208213daa071b49b6974d

cuyler, a. c. (2019). The Role of Foundations in Achieving Creative Justice in the U.S. Cultural Sector. *Grantmakers in the Arts Reader*, *30*(1), p. 6.

cuyler, a. c. (2023). Access, Diversity, Equity, and Inclusion (ADEI) in Cultural Organizations: Challenges and Opportunities. In A. Rhine & J. Pension (Eds.), *Business Issues in the Arts* (pp. 83–104). Routledge.

cuyler, a. c., Linett, E., Yair, K., & McCain, J. (2023). Racial/Ethnic and Gender Diversity in the Orchestra Field in 2023: A Report by the League of American Orchestras. https://americanorchestras.org/racial-ethnic-and-gender-diversity-in-the-orchestra-field-in-2023/

Fogg, B. J. (2024). Fogg Behavior Model. https://behaviormodel.org/

Gilmore, S. (1993). Minorities and Distributional Equity at the National Endowment for the Arts. *Journal of Arts Management, Law, and Society*, *23*(2), pp. 137–173.

Helicon Collaborative. (2017). Not Just Money: Where Is the Money Going? https://medium.com/helicon-collaborative/not-just-money-part-1-abd18e277703?mc_cid=d1e7b15755&mc_eid=4254e9122a

Illinois Commission on the Status of Women. (1985). Report and Recommendations of the Governor and General Assembly Report of the Minority Women's Committee. https://search.alexanderstreet.com/preview/work/bibliographic_entity%7Cbibliographic_details%7C2506947

Kaplan, E. (2023, July 7). The 'American Whitelash' Is Far From Over. *Politico*. https://politico.com/news/magazine/2023/07/02/wes-lowery-whitelash-violence-00104438

Keller, A. (1989). The Arts Manager's Social Responsibility. *Journal of Arts Management, Law, and Society*, *19*(2), pp. 44–54.

Lowery, J. (2023). *American Whitelash: A Changing Nation and the Cost of Progress*. Mariner Books.

Miller, C., & Katz, J. (2024, April 8). What Researchers Discovered When They Sent 80,000 Fake Resumes to U.S. Jobs. *The New York Times*. https://nytimes.com/2024/04/08/upshot/employment-discrimination-fake-resumes.html

National Endowment for the Arts. (2015). When Going Gets Tough: Barriers and Motivations Affecting Arts Attendance. https://arts.gov/sites/default/files/when-going-gets-tough-revised2.pdf

National Endowment for the Humanities. (1965). National Foundation on the Arts and the Humanities Act of 1965 (P. L. No. 89–209). https://neh.gov/about/history/national-foundation-arts-and-humanities-act-1965-pl-89-209

Sidford, H. (2011). Fusing Arts, Culture, and Social Change: High Impact Strategies for Philanthropy. https://ncrp.org/wp-content/uploads/2016/11/Fusing_Arts_Culture_and_Social_Change-1.pdf

Sussman, S. (2024, April 16). A Hidden Sexual-Assault Scandal at the New York Philharmonic. https://vulture.com/article/new-york-philharmonic-sexual-assault-scandal.html

Tsioulcas, A. (2019, February 21). Top Flutist Settles Gender Pay-Gap Suit With Boston Symphony Orchestra. *National Public Radio* (NPR). https://npr.org/2019/02/21/696574690/top-flutist-settles-gender-pay-gap-suit-with-boston-symphony-orchestra#:~:text=Elizabeth%20Rowe%2C%20the%20principal%20flutist,than%20%24200%2C000%20in%20unpaid%20wages

4 Progress on Creative Justice in the U.S. Creative Sector

Case Studies

As I begin this chapter, Frantz Fanon's (2005, p. 145) statement, "Each generation must discover its mission, fulfill it or betray it, in relative opacity" from *The Wretched of the Earth*, rings true to me as a reminder of how low casted peoples inherit the seemingly incessant fight for their civil and human rights. Furthermore, in a 2018 study, I investigated two research questions to assess the quality and quantity of progress cultural organizations made on DEI as revealed through public statements about their short-term goals and practices on their websites. First, what do service arts organizations' DEI statements communicate about their positions on DEI? Second, do service arts organizations hold themselves accountable for achieving DEI in the sector; if so, how? I exclusively focused on service arts organizations in the U.S. because they function as member-driven, nonprofit, professional trade associations that represent arts agencies, arts councils, arts funders, chamber music, dance, museums, opera, symphony, and theater, all key actors within the U.S. creative sector. Arts service organizations' collective efforts demonstrated not only some progress but also some gaps that called into question the verisimilitude of their commitment to achieving DEI within the creative sector (cuyler, 2021). While most arts service organizations in the study appeared well-informed about the need for DEI within the creative sector, two organizations' statements lacked articulation of this critical motivation for engaging in DEI. Some organizations opted to focus on one aspect of DEI as a catchall without explaining why or with regard to the relationships that exist between the three practices, and how they work in concert to actualize *creative justice* for historically and continuously low casted peoples based on their social identities in U.S. society.

That most of the organizations did not hold themselves accountable for achieving DEI or invite their members and/or the public to hold them accountable for practicing DEI indicated the place where confusion, and some 'bullshitting' occurred in these organizations' work due to a lack of competency on leading DEI. In addition, not one of the organizations considered access a critical goal and practice of their work, which compelled me to add it as a short-term goal and practice of the process towards achieving *creative justice*. As a reminder, in Chapters 2 and 3, I articulated the equation for achieving

DOI: 10.4324/9781003246909-4

Table 4.1 Summary of Service Arts Organizations' DEI

Service Arts Organization	*Rationale*	*DEI*	*Accountability*
1. American Alliance of Museums	√	√	1
2. Chamber Music America	√	√	1
3. Stage Directors and Choreographers Society	√	√	1
4. National Assembly of State Arts Agencies	√	√	2
5. Grantmakers in the Arts	√	√	1
6. Americans for the Arts	√	–	2
7. Chorus America	–	√	2
8. Dance/USA	√	–	2
9. League of American Orchestras	√	–	2
10. Theater Communications Group	–	–	3

creative justice as (A)ccess+(D)iversity+(E)quity+(I)nclusion=Creative Justice (CJ). Service arts organizations likely felt pressured by their members and peers to have 'something' vs. having 'nothing', which may explain key gaps in a well-developed ADEI plan that improves climate, culture, and the intentional engagement of human differences within cultural organizations and across the creative sector. As shown in Table 4.1, only four out of ten arts service organizations in the study had a rationale, engaged DEI; and articulated an accountability plan (Cuyler, 2021).

Because of the study's findings, I routinely advise cultural organizations to avoid making ADEI statements if they cannot commit to: (1) defining ADEI for themselves (Telford et al., 2024), (2) articulating a defensible rationale for engaging in ADEI, (3) articulating their goals and how they plan to achieve them, (4) reporting progress on their goals and why they have not achieved them, and lastly (5) inviting public comment and accountability on their stated goals. Since conducting the study, the U.S. has experienced a global pandemic, increased political polarization, and incessant government led attacks on low casted peoples. I have also observed a cyclical and repugnant pattern. In U.S. society and the creative sector, progress often comes at the expense of human life. Sometimes the lives of Black folx, such as Medgar Evers, Malcolm X, Dr. Martin Luther King, Jr., Ahmaud Aurbery, Breonna Taylor, George Floyd, and far too many others. Sometimes, at the expense of White folx' lives. Assassins murdered Presidents Abraham Lincoln and John F. Kennedy, Jr. because of their anti-racist policies abolishing slavery and enshrining civil rights as law for Black Americans. As further evidence of my assertion and observation, I encourage readers to examine the public reaction and discourse following the release of the video of police beating Rodney King and compare it to public reaction and discourse after the release of the video of Derek Chauvin murdering George

Floyd. Keep in mind nearly 30 years passed between these two events. Then, contemplate the question, what changed between the two incidents?

Now, in my examination of progress and maybe transformation within the creative sector, I first want to highlight the proliferation of people hired in professional ADEI roles across the creative sector since 2020 as noteworthy (cuyler, 2023). Before, 2020, I only knew of Makeba Clay serving as the inaugural Chief Diversity Officer at the Philips Collection in such a role with a cultural organization. In fact, most cultural organizations appeared reticent to allocating funds to hire a full-time professional to lead and manage their ADEI-related transformation work. However, in 2020, the Philadelphia Orchestra promoted Doris Parent to Chief Inclusion, Diversity, Equity, Access, Success (IDEAS) Officer, the first such role in U.S. orchestras. In fact, the 2023 League of American Orchestras' conference offered its first EDI constituency, which serve as opportunities for professionals to gather for meetings with peers who serve in similar roles at other orchestras across the country during the conference.

In addition to orchestras, similar positions in dance companies, museums, opera companies, and theater companies emerged across the country. This single change indicates that cultural organizations broadly see ADEI as valuable enough to entrust its care, leadership, and management to a professional in the same way that it has for artistic programming, education, financial management, fundraising, HR, and marketing, among other organizational functions. I encourage continued engagement of this hiring practice because it increases the likelihood that cultural organizations will attempt to lead and manage transformation toward an organizational 'culture of care' to improve climate, culture, and the intentional engagement of human difference in pursuit of *creative justice*. Cultural organizations that singularly entrust their ADEI to a board committee or taskforce struggle to initiate, lead, manage, and sustain this critical work toward *creative justice*, though such an arrangement may work, if led by a member of the staff. Smaller cultural organizations might consider re-structuring staff duties to include ADEI work so that it does not fall off their radars. Furthermore, hiring ADEI professionals in cultural organizations has crystalized and held steady now across the creative sector over the last four years that arts leadership and management degree programs should offer a required class teaching students how to lead and manage ADEI in cultural organizations in their curricula like arts and community engagement, cultural policy, financial management, fundraising, and marketing and audience development, among other cognates.

American Alliance of Museums

Completing the foundational work of having a rationale, fully engaging DEI, and articulating an accountability plan positioned the American Alliance of Museums (AAM) very well to lead its members in DEAI, and anti-racism.

In addition to providing members with a digital resource library (American Alliance of Museums, 2024), the service arts organization has broadly encouraged the integration of DEAI regarding the board, collections, and staff. Most outstanding, in 2022, AAM announced a multi-year initiative to transform the standards that guide best practices and accreditation for museums by embedding DEAI more explicitly, a suggestion for which I have emphatically advocated (American Alliance of Museums, 2022; Cuyler, 2020). Once completed, this transformation will require AAM's 35,000 accredited museums, and any other museum that pursues accreditation in the future, to demonstrate how it practices DEAI to receive accreditation. As a tool from which all cultural organizations can learn and adapt, Sweeney et al. (2022) articulated the prioritization of DEAI strategies in Table 4.2 by asking museum directors, "how much of a priority is each of the following equity, diversity, and inclusion strategies at your museum?" "In addition, by defining it and providing a toolkit in support of it, AAM has guided and supported their members in measuring their social impact" (Mileham & Johnson, 2023), as well as a free survey to help their members measure belonging at museums (Price & Applebaum, 2022). Social impact and belonging add critical dimensions that enable AAM and museums to own and personalize their ADEI narratives in pursuit of *creative justice*.

Unlike the AAM, the performing arts service arts organizations for composers, choruses, dance companies, opera, orchestras, and theater do not have accreditation as a power that they can wield to compel their members to

Table 4.2 DEAI Strategies in Museums

DEAI Strategy
Ensuring pay equity for employees in comparable positions
Providing a livable wage for all employees and contractors
Providing internal training for staff addressing equity, diversity, and inclusion issues
Ensuring the museum is accessible to visitors with disabilities
Increasing the diversity of the content and program positions (i.e., curatorial and education positions)
Altering acquisition strategies to add works by historically underrepresented artists
Providing public programming geared toward historically underrepresented audiences
Increasing the diversity of the board of trustees
Increasing the diversity of staff in senior management positions
Digitizing and making broadly available artworks by historically underrepresented artists
Hosting loan exhibitions of artworks by historically underrepresented artists
Increasing the diversity of museum volunteers
Interrogating the institution's history of relations with marginalized communities
Providing public programming designed to advance social justice
Deaccessioning and/or repatriating collection items in collaboration with communities of origin (original communities/community members from whom material artifacts were acquired, as well as their descendants)

embrace and practice ADEI in pursuit of *creative justice*. Still, these organizations have made progress worthy of attention, especially for those searching for ideas of how and where to begin ADEI. Again, cultural organizations should practice ADEI to achieve *creative justice* by improving the creative sector's climate, culture, and intentional engagement of people across the vastness of human differences. As a measure of accountability, the creative sector and cultural organizations should measure progress on climate, culture, and intentional engaging of human difference, and share and discuss their progress publicly. Doing so not only maintains communication with the public about progress but also builds trust with communities.

American Composers Forum

In 2021, American Composer Forum's (ACF's) president and CEO, Vanessa Rose, board co-chair, Stephen Miles, and I proposed to present a panel entitled, "The American Composers Forum: Creative Justice as Transformational Process" at the Social Theory, Politics & the Arts (STP&A) conference in Sarasota, Florida. The presentation intended to share ACF's work as an example of the *creative justice* theory and practice in action. Unfortunately, the Delta variant of COVID-19 caused the cancellation of the conference. Co-developing the proposal with Steve and Vanessa allowed me to learn about ACF's racial equity work. I also recently joined ACF's board. Though founded in 1973, ACF committed to becoming an anti-racist organization in 2020. As a way of recalibrating their work, ACF re-considered their basic assumptions, including the term 'composer', which some view as inherently exclusionary. In fact, one of the advocacy goals that ACF aspires to achieve, as expressed in their *Statement of Commitment to Racial Equity*, is to "expand and illustrate the multiple ways the term 'composer' can be applied and include language that is not limited to 'composer', e.g., music creators, creative musicians, artists, etc." (American Composers Forum, 2024a).

ACF developed their statement over an 18-month process with focus groups and public forums that build on critical race theory (CRT), as well as other resources shared within the statement (Rose, 2021). In her reflections on their work after the first year, Rose (2021) wrote, "We have achieved success, learned from failures, and discussed policies and decisions that challenge our assumptions". Rose's statement provides the creative sector a sense of what to expect when pursuing organizational transformation that centers *creative justice*.

ACF's *Statement of Commitment to Racial Equity* boldly articulated achieving a majority Black, Indigenous, and People of Color (BIPOC) – or at 60% – representation throughout the organization by their 50th anniversary in 2025. ACF also seeks to include within the racial equity frame diverse gender identities, musical approaches and perspectives, ages, (dis)abilities, cultures, religions, backgrounds, sexual orientations, and broad definitions of 'American'. The statement/strategic plan also articulated three pillars of ACF's work, which includes (1) supporting artists, (2) advocacy, and (3) leading by example. The glossary of terms included and the flexibility to change it as ACF continues its learning and transformation also empowers the organization to own its narrative about its work (American Composers Forum, 2024a). At the end of her 2021 reflections, Rose stated, "This is our report card to you, our community, about our first year of this endeavor. We will continue to release these reports on an annual basis and invite you to question, comment on, and keep us accountable to our equity promises". ACF has consistently used the report card to publicly report on and share its progress toward achieving its goals, and *creative justice* for music creators historically and continuously low casted in U.S. society because of their social identities (American Composers Forum, 2024a; American Composers Forum, 2024b).

Chorus America

In 2018, Chorus America articulated DEI as important, but they did not have a clear rationale for using these practices, nor did they invite their members and the public to hold them accountable for achieving the aims of the short-term goals and practices. I have observed Chorus America's ADEI organizational transformation work autoethnographically through participant observation because of the strategic planning work that I facilitated with them in 2022, but also because I served as a faculty member of their management institute, facilitated four iterations of their Racial ADEI Lab for white identifying choral leaders (Chorus America, 2024a), co-facilitated one iteration of their Choral Executive Leadership Academy for global majority choral leaders (Chorus America, 2024b), and led a plenary on anti-racism at their 2023 conference in San Francisco, California, as well as presented at their online conference in 2020 and 2021. While their mission and guiding principles warrant readers' study, I highlight their vision here, which is, "Chorus America envisions a vibrant society in which diverse singing communities affirm and share the full range and depth of our humanity". Using choral singing as the bridge, Chorus America aims to harness the power of singing to bring people together. The service arts organization for choruses has been so courageous in serving their members through ADEI that I often joke with them that they should develop a program called, "Sing for Democracy". In doing so, they could test the power of choral singing to bring people together across political tribes, especially given that their chorus impact study found that people who sing in choirs engage more civically through contributing financially, volunteering, and voting than the general public (Grunwald Associates, LLC & Chorus America, 2019).

Though I could write extensively about the programs for global majority and white choral leaders, from my perspective, they remain strong programs because they aim to educate people, and not simply to train them. I have enjoyed the deep dives into U.S. history that the attendees and I have taken in our sessions holding each other in tremendous care while doing so.

Also, the proactive strategic response practicing that the lab offers via case study learning. For example, learning that Handel, the composer of the *Messiah*, invested in the transatlantic slave trade remains a thought-provoking ethical case because the oratorio generates a great deal of revenue for choirs. Ultimately, the lab reminds me that ADEI education has the potential to aid, inform, and sustain organizational transformation. I also remember attendees' gratitude for having an opportunity to continue learning difficult content that they need to know to improve their individual and organizational ADEI short-term goals and practices with bravery and courage. In addition, my co-facilitator of the Choral Executive Leadership Academy for global majority choral leaders, Arreon Harley-Emerson, and I could not have anticipated the impact that partnering with attendees to develop personalized professional plans would have on aiding them in discovering the variety of capital that they bring with them into predominantly white, as well as predominantly global majority choral spaces when we planned the curriculum.

League of American Orchestras

I also know the League of American Orchestras' work autoethnographically because I co-authored the *Racial/Ethnic and Gender Diversity in the Orchestra Field in 2023* report (cuyler et al., 2023). I have also facilitated two professional development sessions for their staff and board. As stated earlier, I advise my clients to avoid making ADEI statements if they cannot commit to: (1) defining ADEI for the organization (Telford et al., 2024), (2) articulating a defensible rationale for engaging in ADEI, (3) articulating their goals and how they plan to achieve them, (4) reporting progress on their goals and why they have not achieved them, and (5) inviting public comment and accountability on their stated goals. Though, one could ask why the League had not made more progress after its 1993 report, *Americanizing the American Orchestra*, and the acquittal of the police who violently attacked Rodney King (National Taskforce, 1993), the League's (2020) *Statement on Racial Discrimination* changed my mind. I highlight the following passages:

> Through *listening* to underrepresented voices in our field; centering equity, diversity, and inclusion (EDI) in our programs and convenings; and researching our shared history and heritage, the League of American Orchestras is developing an understanding of the breadth and depth of systemic racial inequities that exist in the orchestra field. The current pandemic and the growing recognition of disproportionate police violence against Black people shine a light on America's long history of systemic inequities for the Black community. This history includes chattel slavery, Black Code and Jim Crow laws, redlining, school segregation, voter suppression, and the prison-industrial complex. This challenging history and the current environment make it essential for us to assert our *deepening*

> *commitment* to be an advocate for and a *credible partner* with Black people and associated organizations as we seek a more equitable and diverse future. . . . The League of American Orchestras *acknowledges, accepts responsibility for, and apologizes* for the role it has played in perpetuating, excusing, and participating in systemic discrimination based on race within the orchestral field. The impacts of our actions have included *the loss of valuable musical and other creative contributions by generations of Black people*. The League recognizes the existence of many forms of discrimination in America that hurt our fellow human beings. In additional to race, these include discrimination based on ethnicity, age, sex, sexual orientation, gender identity, disability, religion, and socio-economic status.

In terms of accountability, the League (2020) agreed to:

> (1) match their commitment with financial resources by allocating 10% of their budget (about $700,000) to equity, diversity, and inclusion (EDI) and anti-racism work both internally and on behalf of members, (2) support and advance orchestras' anti-racism and EDI work by holding essential field-wide conversations that identify and challenge the systems that perpetuate discrimination, fostering learning and action through peer dialogue, providing access to professional EDI expertise, as we currently do through their Catalyst Fund, and growing and updating their EDI Resource Center, (3) model the change they envision by creating an inclusive culture, building systems that support racial equity, and further diversifying their staff and board; (4) build sustained capacity across their organization by engaging professional expertise and starting this fall with ongoing anti-racism training for staff and board and updating their strategy; (5) pursue collective action and partnerships with the AFM, ICSOM, ROPA, and other organizations to advance racial equity practices across the full spectrum of people in orchestras, as they have done as a founding partner of the National Alliance for Audition Support; and (6) address discrimination in orchestras against all underrepresented members of their community by centering the voices of Black and other underrepresented artists and leaders in their National Conference, ongoing learning events, and across advocacy and communications platforms, including Symphony magazine (League of American Orchestras, 2020).

Similarly to ACF's *Statement of Commitment to Racial Equity*, the League's *Statement on Racial Discrimination* does an excellent job of reminding the creative sector that no one should have to "wait their turn for *creative justice*". In addition, in 2013, Dworkin suggested that orchestras should commit 5% of their budgets to inclusion initiatives. The League committed to allocating 10%, doubling Dworkin's suggestion (Dworkin, 2013; League, 2020). The League also offers its members the catalyst fund to help them financially prepare for the budgetary shifts that can cause some cultural organizations to shrink away from pursuing *creative justice* enabled by equity, diversity, and inclusion. I appreciate Flagg's (2020) historical analysis that shows how the orchestral field deeply embedded anti-Black racism into it. Like AAM, the League provides an equity, diversity, and inclusion digital resource center with case studies (League of American Orchestras, 2024) to help its members think holistically and strategically about how to lead and manage organizational transformation toward *creative justice*.

OPERA America

As a current board member of OPERA America, presenter at its conference three times, and delegate of the World Opera Forum, I also have familiarity with the organization's *creative justice*-related work autoethnographically. If the statement, "put your money where your mouth is" rings true, then OPERA America deserves credit for allocating 49.6% of its budget to EDI (M. Scorca, personal communication, February 29, 2024). In addition to allocating ten times as much as Dworkin's 5% suggestion, OPERA America has made progress toward enabling *creative justice*. Notably, in 2018, I did not include the service arts organization in the study because it did not have an ADEI statement publicly available on its website, nor a rationale for why it practices ADEI, or a mechanism for its members and the public to hold the organization accountable for practicing ADEI. Today, however, OPERA America uplifts gender parity (OPERA America, 2024c), LGBTQIA+ equity, and racial justice; including networks that function similarly to affinity groups for these three historically and continuously low casted populations in the U.S. The service arts organization also developed community guidelines and co-developed an anti-discrimination and anti-harassment policy template with the American Guild of Musical Artists (AGMA) to support its members in abating for and decreasing instances of discrimination and harassment (OPERA America, 2024a). I especially appreciate OPERA America compelling its members to participate in conversations about serious issues of concern in opera, for example, Blackface and Yellowface in casting in its magazine. OPERA America, too, offers its members grant programs for civic practice, IDEAS, women conductors and stage directors, and women composers. Lastly, OPERA America's Racial Justice Opera Forum facilitated by its social justice advisor, Quodesia Johnson, remains instrumental in providing the continuing education needed to aid opera's anti-racist transformation for all its members, but especially for people of the global majority. The 2024 forum focused on strengthening commitment, connection and healing, and collective action (OPERA America, 2024b; d).

Youth Orchestras of San Antonio

In 2002, Oldenburg articulated the concept of "third places", or neutral public places where people gather intentionally to interact (Oldenburg, 2002). Different from first places (home) or second places (work) for adults, and first places (home) and second places (school) for young people, third places can include churches, gyms, restaurants, and yoga studios, among others. Given that cultural organizations can serve as third places for adults, they can and should serve as third places for young people, too. I encouraged Youth Orchestras of San Antonio (YOSA) to adopt a "for kids, by kids" ethos and practice to combat adultism. In Chapter 1, I defined adultism as age-based human suffering that impacts young people. In the U.S., I consider people under age 40 young because the Age Discrimination in Employment Act (ADEA) of 1967 only prohibits discrimination against people aged 40 and above. Employers can and often do discriminate against people under age 40 by telling them that they do not have enough experience, which of course directly correlates to age, a characteristic that they cannot change about themselves. With cultural organizations whose missions center school-aged youth, then, adultism can easily become an embedded and hidden ethos and practice that constrains the cultural engagement, flourishing, practices, values, and thereby, *creative justice* of young people.

Because arts education in public schools remains in a perpetual state of decline, I advised YOSA to provide a holistic arts education by opening the entire orchestral experience on and behind the stage to young people. Thus, I encouraged YOSA to proactively engage young people in co-curating the youth orchestra experience as a creative third place. To act on this recommendation, I encouraged YOSA to combat adultism by inviting young people to participate in the youth orchestra not only as players and/or audience members but in all the positionalities that I identified in Chapter 3 including artists (composers, conductors, production, etc.), board members, donors/funders, partners, staff, vendors, and volunteers. If Ericsson et al. (2007) correctly identified 'deliberate practice' as the gateway to developing expertise, then YOSA will maximize the power of arts education by enabling young people to fully participate in orchestras without constraints by enabling their deliberate practice of fully engaging in youth orchestras, thus actualizing their *creative justice*.

Gender Equity Index

Since 2020's summer of racial discontent, cultural organizations across the creative sector have produced reports revealing the status of representational diversity in dance (Dance Data Project, 2024), museums (Sweeney et al., 2022), opera (OPERA America, 2022), and orchestras (cuyler et al., 2023). The Dance Data Project recently announced the results of its first-ever *Gender Equity Index* (GEI) to assess how ballet companies measure up in terms of commissioning female creators, promoting women to leadership positions, and fostering a transparent and accountable culture through the completion of the GEI survey. Ranking the largest 50 ballet companies with a few omissions, DDP developed three categories based on scores that include *Needs Work* (0–30%), *Good* (30%–50%), and *Exceptional* (50%–100%). In addition to helping ballet companies see clearly where they can make improvements, the GEI provides companies with a snapshot of how they compare with their peers. According to DDP (2024), "Though a woman dominated field (76.6%), men continue to hold more prestigious and higher-paying positions such as artistic and executive directors and receive the most lucrative and high-profile commissions as choreographers". The GEI skillfully and publicly reports on who gets the most highly valued opportunities to incentivize change in ballet. The creative sector needs more such annual indexes, especially to encourage cultural organizations to continue their organizational transformation toward *creative justice*.

Continuum on Becoming an Anti-racist Arts and Cultural Organization

In 2015, Hsieh first developed her *Continuum on Becoming An Anti-racist Arts and Cultural Organization* for the Racial Equity Arts Lab Forum (REAL Forum) based on an adaptation by Crossroads Ministry, Chicago, Illinois, from a Multicultural Organization Development theory by Bailey Jackson and Rita Hardiman. At the time, the creative sector and the cultural organizations that comprised it likely did not realize just how much it would come to need this critical tool to chart a path toward becoming an anti-racist cultural organization. The tool highlights six organizational culture types and key behaviors that regularly occur within cultural organizations to sustain an anti-racist culture (Table 4.3). As with all tools, readers should avoid reductionism in applying the tool to their assessment of their organizational culture because of the ways in which the external environment (cultural, demographic, economic, educational, legal/political, and technological), dynamics, people, and power differentials complexly impact organizational culture, which can include attitudes, behaviors, customs, norms, policies, practices, and procedures. Still, I have used this tool to help cultural organizations and their workers to better understand their organizational culture and the actions that they needed to take to transform their cultures. The tool has also helped cultural organizations to understand not only where they are but also where they aspire to go, and the commitment it will take to get where they aspire to ultimately end up. Hsieh updated the Continuum I present next on April 28, 2022 (K. Hsieh, personal communication, March 18, 2024).

Through my examination of ADEI currently occurring across the U.S. creative sector, I have identified ten interventions that show potential for aiding the creative sector's transformation toward achieving *creative justice* by developing a 'culture of care' through its climate, culture, and intentional engagement of people across the vastness of human difference (Woods, 2024). This cursory examination does not purport to comprehensively study all practices.

Table 4.3 Continuum on Becoming an Anti-Racist Arts and Cultural Organization

Racial & cultural differences seen as deficits		*Tolerant of racial and cultural differences*		*Racial and cultural differences seen as assets*	
1. Exclusive Segregated Organization	**2. Passive Status Quo Organization**	**3. Symbolic Multicultural Organization**	**4. Evolving Anti-Racist Institution**	**5. Structurally Changing Organization**	**6. Inclusive Transformed Organization**
1. Intentionally and publicly excludes or segregates People of the Global Majority – PGM* 2. Intentionally and publicly enforces the racist status quo throughout institution 3. Institutionalization of racism includes formal policies and practices, teachings and decision-making on all levels 4. Usually has similar intentional policies and practices toward other socially oppressed groups, such as women, people who are disabled, elderly and	1. Tolerant of a limited number of PGM with "proper" perspective and credentials 2. May still secretly limit or exclude people of the global majority in contradiction to public policies 3. Continues to intentionally maintain white power and privilege through its formal policies and practices, teachings and decision-making on all levels of institutional life	1. Has public statement committing to diversity, equity and inclusion but hasn't implemented changes embodying aspirations 2. Carries out intentional inclusive-ness efforts, recruiting "someone of color" on committees or staff 3. Expanding view of diversity includes other socially oppressed groups, such as women, people who are disabled, elders, youth, LGBTQ+, immigrants, etc. 4. Might see themselves as "color-blind" in hiring, programming, marketing 5. Marketing materials and website include higher %	1. Growing understanding of racism and other -isms as barriers 2. Develops analysis of systemic racism and other oppressions 3. Board/staff participate in on-going anti-racism training 4. New consciousness of institutiona-lized white power/privilege 5. Develops intentional identity as an "antiracist" institution 6. Begins to develop accountability to racially oppressed communities 7. Increasing commitment to dismantle racism and eliminate inherent white advantage, but – 8. Institutional structures and culture that maintain white power and privilege	1. Commits to process of intentional institutional restructuring, based on anti-racist analysis and identity 2. Embracing a more collective culture 3. Audits and restructures organizational culture to ensure full participation of PGM intersectionally & including their worldview, culture & working styles 4. PGM are included in all levels of the organization from board to leadership to staff to artists 5. Implements structures, policies and practices with participatory deci-sion-making and other forms of power sharing at all levels of org 6. Commits to dismantle racism in the wider community,	1. Full participation and shared power with people across all races and social spectrums in creating, deciding and implementing its vision, mission, values, structure, constituency, policies and practices 2. Those who have been most impacted by systemic oppression are centered and decide individually how they want to participate 3. Transformational Relational Culture rather than Transactional Individualistic one 4. Collective org structure 5. Functions from an asset-based framework 6. Instills a sense of joy, trust and gratitude among all

(*Continued*)

Table 4.3 (Continued)

children, people who identify as queer, immigrants, etc. 5. Upholds White Supremacy culture *** People of the Global Majority (PGM)** is an emerging, collective and universally inclusive term encompassing people who are Black, Indigenous, Asian, Pacific Islander, Latina/o/x, multi-racial, MENA (Middle East and North Africa), creating greater connection, solidarity and empowerment for the people who represent over 80% of the world's population. **POC**: Used mostly in the U.S., this acronym	4. Often declares, "We don't have a problem" or is fine with or isn't even aware of having an all-white or predominantly white organization 5. No outreach is done at any level to diversify the organization or they are doing outreach for "everyone" and can't help it if only white people respond 6. Programming is centered on white artists, Western European art-forms and white cultural values	people of color than exist in organization 6. Primary strategy for reaching communities of color is offering discounted opportunities or scholarships 7. Primary strategy for hiring is to include a statement about encouraging POC to apply 8. Can't understand why PGM haven't responded to their efforts 9. Possible White-Savior complex - the organization feels like they're helping PGM by offering them opportunities 10. PGM still perceived through a deficit-framework	still intact and relatively untouched 9. Those in decision-making positions may still be predominantly white or hold onto white cultural values even if more of the artists and supporting staff include PGM or PGM leader is only allowed to be the face of the org 10. Programming includes one or two annual "diversity" slots 11. Double standards in how people of color and their artwork are viewed, marketed and included 12. Extra burden might be placed on PGM artists/staff that aren't expected of White staff, even if un-intentional (expecting them to be cultural consultants, translate materials, represent entire communities, outreach to their communities) without	and builds clear lines of accountability to all oppressed communities 7. Reaches out to involve PGM communities for all programming, not just the racially specific ones 8. Anti-racist multicultural diversity becomes an institutional asset 9. Examines & disrupts anti-Blackness 10. Works in solidarity with other PGM & oppressed communities 11. Redefines and rebuilds all relationships and activities in society, based on anti-racist values 12. Seeks deeper awareness in contributing to a more racially equitable, intersectional and human-centered workplace 13. Acceptance of honest and direct feedback while holding compassion and grace for each person	7. Inspires growth and learning 8. Adaptive and continually evolving 9. A place of possibility 10. Each person involved with the very diverse organization (board, staff, artists, supporters, collaborators, audience) has agency and feels welcomed, included, seen, heard and valued for the full spectrum of their humanity 11. Everyone is able to show up authentically and work to their fullest potential 12. Every person feels alive and transformed 13. Shared sense of community, trust and mutual care within the organization and its broader community where everyone has each other's back & respect

(*Continued*)

Table 4.3 (Continued)

for People of Color is a term that includes people who are Black, Indigenous, Asian, Pacific Islander, Latina/o/x, multi-racial, MENA (Middle East and North Africa). **BIPOC**: A more recent evolution of the term POC referring to Black, Indigenous, and People of Color. Primarily used in the U.S. to highlight the unique struggles and significant disparities that Black and Indigenous people have experienced in this country.	7. The inclusion of PGM artists is perceived as lowering the quality of the art 8. PGM audiences aren't viewed as worth the effort either because they believe that the cost to reach them isn't worth the return or that they wouldn't "fit" or might make the regular patrons feel uncomfortable or even scare away the long-time supporters 9. Fear that the inclusion of PGM art will result in a loss of support from their donors	11. Sees itself as "non-racist" institution – "We're open to all people," but – 12. "Not to those who make waves" 13. Little or no contextual change in culture, policies and decision-making 14. Is still relatively unaware of continuing patterns of privilege, paternalism and control 15. White cultural norms are centered 16. White fragility shows up when PGM or other oppressed folx share about their experience 17. Generic, performative, check-box equity work rather than specific, action-oriented engagement	additional compensation, budget or support 13. PGM may be gaining more access to the organization but they still experience significant harm 14. Organization functions on White cultural norms so PGM have to code switch to fit in or be perceived as "professional" enough 15. PGM feel like they need to navigate the unpredictability of an organization striving to be "woke" but not actually there yet so when an invisible line is crossed it's usually the PGM who have to back track rather than the non-PGM willing to lean in	14. Space, time & resources provided 15. Caucus spaces based on identity/positionality as deemed by those with least perceived power 16. PGM staff, board members, artists and supporters are valued for the expertise they share as full human beings and not just for their race 17. Collaborates with & compensates PGM folx in an equitable way, centering their voices, leadership, ideas, and needs in the process 18. Honors multi-dimensionality of PGM people	14. Multi-cultural Audiences see themselves reflected in the work, staff & artists, and feel humanized by the depiction 15. Those being depicted in the artistic work are involved in its creation at a decision-making level 16. Public feels collective ownership in the organization and is able to voice authentic feedback that is truly listened to and taken into consideration for future planning 17. Organization allies with others in creating true liberation for all people

Updated 4/28/22. Created for arts & cultural groups by Kathy Hsieh for Racial Equity Arts Lab Forum (REAL Forum) © based on an adaptation by Crossroads Ministry, Chicago, IL, © from a Multicultural Organization Development theory authored by Bailey Jackson and Rita Hardiman ©.

Nor does it assess where any of the organizations profiled in this chapter will ultimately end up on their ADEI journeys. While the snapshots in time indicate room for expansion and growth, I applaud the progress made over the last four years and encourage its continuation. I also challenge the creative sector to consider how it might amplify and hasten the pursuit of sectoral transformation through collaboration instead of competition. Clearly, the creative sector has borrowed many of the interventions from the for-profit corporate sector. Though cultural organizations have had to do significant work to adapt the interventions to their environments, if they yield the desired transformation, then that indicates that the intervention works for them. Sharing interventions that work could prove especially beneficial. Table 4.4 shows an inventory of the interventions examined in this chapter and the organization profiled that uses the intervention.

Table 4.4 Cultural Organizations' Use of ADEI Interventions

ADEI Intervention	*Cultural Organizations Profiled*
1. Accreditation	American Alliance of Museums
2. ADEI professionals	American Alliance of Museums, League of American Orchestras, OPERA America, Youth Orchestras of San Antonio
3. Affinity groups	American Alliance of Museums, League of American Orchestras, OPERA America
4. Annual reporting on ADEI	American Composers Forum
5. Assessments, evaluation, and research	American Alliance of Museums, League of American Orchestras, OPERA America, Gender Equity Index, and Continuum on Becoming an Anti-racist Arts and Cultural Organization
6. Budgetary allocations	American Alliance of Museums, American Composers Forum, Chorus America, League of American Orchestras, OPERA America, Youth Orchestras of San Antonio
7. Education/professional development	American Alliance of Museums, American Composers Forum, Chorus America, League of American Orchestras, OPERA America, Youth Orchestras of San Antonio
8. Digital educational resources	American Alliance of Museums, Chorus America, League of American Orchestras, OPERA America
9. Funding and grant opportunities	American Alliance of Museums, American Composers Forum, Chorus America, League of American Orchestras, OPERA America
10. Strategic Planning	American Alliance of Museums, American Composers Forum, Chorus America, Youth Orchestras of San Antonio, Gender Equity Index, and Continuum on Becoming an Anti-Racist Arts and Cultural Organization

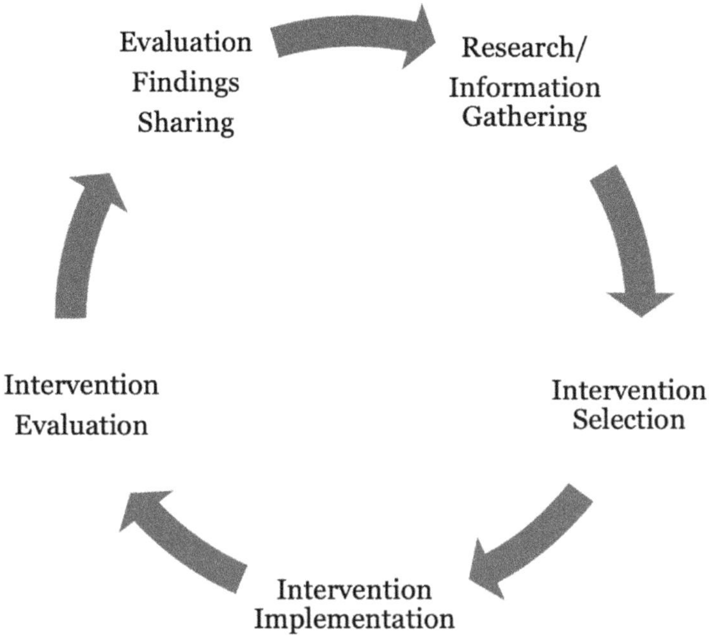

Figure 4.1 The Cycle of ADEI Intervention Selection Toward Creative Justice.

Figure 4.1 shows the cyclical process that I have observed cultural organizations lead and manage using the interventions identified in this chapter to achieve *creative justice*. To ensure that *creative justice* becomes a part of their culture at a cellular level so that no transition of a board president, CEO, or executive director can threaten or weaken the work, cultural organizations should re-assess their climates, cultures, and intentional engagement of people across the vastness of human difference at the three, five, seven, and ten years marks to adjust as needed. After then, I strongly encourage annual assessments to make sure that the chosen interventions continue to have their desired outcomes. Cultural organizations should also commit to making this organizational transformation work apart of their organizational operations in the same ways that they have made artistic programming, community engagement, education, financial management, fundraising, HR, and marketing. Indeed, communities change and cultural organizations must remain aware of how their community has changed to ensure and protect their community members' *creative justice*.

I have also observed an innovation occurring in practice worthy of mention in this chapter. As the Venn diagram in Figure 4.2 shows, many cultural organizations increasingly understand their ADEI, community engagement,

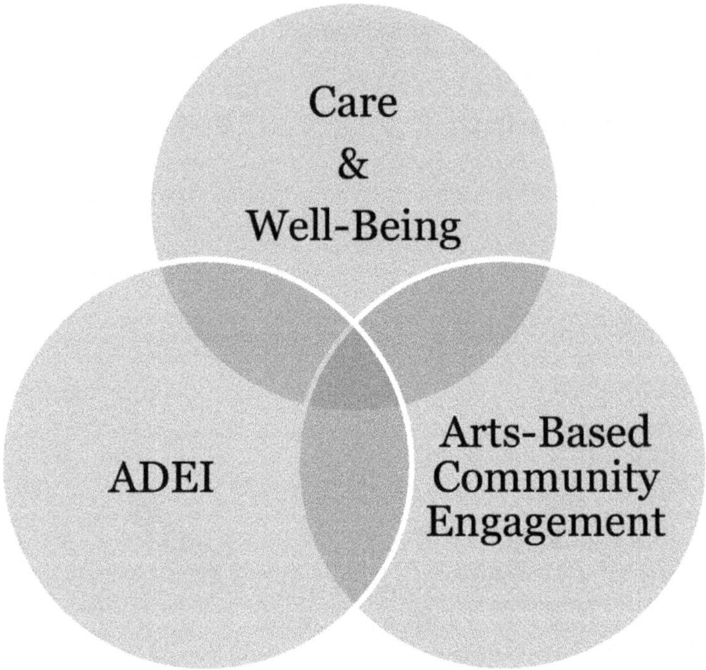

Figure 4.2 The Convergence of ADEI, Community Engagement, and Well-Being.

and well-being work converging as their 'culture of care'. San Francisco Opera, for example, calls this diversity, equity, and community (DEC) (San Francisco Opera, 2024). The overlapping areas highlight the potential sweet spot of cultural organizations' transformation work. Based on my observations, organizations that show that they care about people have less difficulty stimulating and sustaining the climate and culture that they desire.

In closing, Haynes (2024) raised the question, when pursuing ADEI organizational transformation where should organizations start, with people or culture? Ideally, organizations should start with culture, but what if the organization lacks the critical mass or moral courage to use power to compel transformation? Furthermore, what if the organization does not know that it needs to transform? Who or what compels transformation? Likely, many organizations exist in this state, which explains why the U.S. creative sector has too few good models to which it can point to as examples. Still, the creative sector must find a way to lead and manage climate, culture, and the intentional engagement of people across the vastness of human differences in pursuit of ADEI simultaneously. Depending on the level of resistance from within the organization, it could take an organization three to five years or longer to fully implement the transformation. Sustaining the transformation, however, I hypothesize that it takes 10 years based on my observations. But this ensures cementing the transformation at a cellular level so that it becomes the organization's new mode of operandi in perpetuity.

In this chapter, I examined the AAM, ACF, Chorus America, League of American Orchestras, and OPERA America's use of ADEI to improve their climate, culture, and intentional engagement of people across the vastness of human difference toward *creative justice*. I also discussed the YOSA's work tackling adultism to develop a creative third place for young people. In addition, I offered the Dance Data Project's *Gender Equity Index* and Kathy Hsieh's *Continuum on Becoming an Anti-Racist Arts and Cultural Organization* as examples of tools that can assist cultural organizations in improving their climate and culture to advance *creative justice*. In Chapter 5, I will offer a brief review of Chapters 1 through 4. I will interrogate current attacks on ADEI to further bolster my argument for shifting the long-term goal to *creative justice*. Lastly, I will suggest a research agenda that practitioners and scholars should collaboratively investigate to identify and further conceptualize evidence-based approaches to enable the U.S. creative sector in achieving *creative justice*.

References

American Alliance of Museums. (2022). Diversity, Equity to Become Required for Museum Accreditation, Standards. https://aam-us.org/2022/10/17/diversity-equity-to-become-required-for-museum-accreditation-standards/

American Alliance of Museums. (2024). Diversity, Equity, Accessibility, Inclusion (DEAI), & Anti-Racism. https://aam-us.org/topic/diversity-equity-accessibility-inclusion-anti-racism/

American Composers Forum. (2024a). Statement of Commitment on Racial Equity. https://composersforum.org/about/racial-equity-statement/

American Composers Forum. (2024b). Racial Equity Report Card. https://composersforum.org/artist-equity/racial-equity-report-card/

Chorus America. (2024a). ADEI Learning Lab. https://chorusamerica.org/adei-learning-lab

Chorus America. (2024b). Choral Executive Leadership Academy. https://chorusamerica.org/leadership-academy

cuyler, a. c. (2020). Looking Beyond What We've Done Before: Minding Potential Blind Spots in Diversifying U.S. Museums. *International Journal of the Inclusive Museum*, *13*(4), pp. 39–46.

cuyler, a. c. (2021). Diversity, Equity, and Inclusion (DEI) Statements in the U.S. Creative Sector: Progress, or More Bullshit? *Cultural Management: Science and Education*, *5*(2), pp. 33–46.

cuyler, a. c. (2023). Access, Diversity, Equity, and Inclusion (ADEI) in Cultural Organizations: Challenges and Opportunities. In A. Rhine & J. Pension (Eds.), *Business Issues in the Arts* (pp. 83–104). Routledge.

cuyler, a. c., Linett, E., & Yair, K. (2023). Racial/Ethnic and Gender Diversity in the Orchestra Field in 2023. https://americanorchestras.org/racial-ethnic-and-gender-diversity-in-the-orchestra-field-in-2023/

Dance Data Project (DDP). (2024). Gender Equity Index. https://dancedata-project.com/gender-equity-index/

Dworkin, A. (2013). Inclusion in American Orchestras. *Grantmakers in the Arts (GIA) Reader*, *25*(1). https://giarts.org/article/inclusion-american-orchestras

Ericsson, K., Prietula, M., & Cokely, E. (2007, July–August). The Making of an Expert. *Harvard Business Review*. https://hbr.org/2007/07/the-making-of-an-expert

Fanon, F. (2005). *The Wretched of the Earth*. Grove Press.

Flagg, A. (2020, Summer). Anti-Black Discrimination in American Orchestras. *Symphony Magazine*. https://americanorchestras.org/wp-content/uploads/2021/01/Anti-Black-Discrimination-in-American-Orchestras.pdf

Grunwald Associates, LLC and Chorus America. (2019). The Chorus Impact Study: Singing for a Lifetime. https://chorusamerica.org/resource/chorus-impact-study-singing-lifetime

Haynes, E. (2024, May 16). 'Start With Culture Change': The Work Boards Must Do Before Launching Diversity Efforts. *The Chronicle of Philanthropy*. https://philanthropy.com/article/start-with-culture-change-the-work-boards-must-do-before-launching-diversity-efforts?utm_source=Iterable&utm_medium=email&utm_campaign=campaign_9875843_nl_Philanthropy-Today_date_20240516&cid=pt&source=&sourceid=&sra=true

Hsieh, K. (2022). Continuum on Becoming an Anti-Racist Arts and Cultural Organization. https://docs.google.com/document/d/1XoxVbg7LqDOw8viYgSULMYGGcLVl1Kj1r51vTGFq48k/edit

League of American Orchestras. (2020). Statement on Racial Discrimination. https://americanorchestras.org/a-new-statement-on-racial-discrimination-august-2020/

League of American Orchestras. (2024). Equity, Diversity, and Inclusion Resource Center. https://americanorchestras.org/learn/equity-diversity-and-inclusion/

Mileham, M., & Johnson, E. (2023, September 8). A Toolkit to Measure Your Museum's Social Impact. https://aam-us.org/2023/09/08/a-toolkit-to-measure-your-museums-social-impact/?utm_source=American+Alliance+of+Museums&utm_campaign=40c290a1af-FieldNotes_2023_Sep11&utm_medium=email&utm_term=0_-40c290a1af-%5BLIST_EMAIL_ID%5D

National Taskforce. (1993). Americanizing the American Orchestra. https://americanorchestras.org/wp-content/uploads/2021/01/americanizing-the-american-orchestra.pdf

Oldenburg, R. (2002). *Celebrating the Third Place: Inspiring Stories About the "Great Good Places" at the Heart of Our Communities*. Da Capo Press.

OPERA America. (2022). Field-Wide Opera Demographic Report 2021. https://operaamerica.org/r/business-research/8569/2021-field-wide-opera-demographic-report

OPERA America. (2024a). Policy on Anti-Discrimination, Anti-Harassment and a Respectful and Inclusive Workplace. https://operaamerica.org/industry-resources/#eyJxIjoiIiwidG9waWNzIjpbXSwiY29udGVudFRjowLCJmcm9tIjpudWxsLCJ0byI6bnVsbCwicGFnZSI6MSwicGFnZVNpemUiOjI0LCJ2aWV3IjoxLCJtYWdQYWdlIjoxLCJtYWdQY-

WdlU2l6ZSI6MjQsIm1hZ2F6aW5lIjpmYWxzZSwibG9hZFRvcGl-jUGlucyI6dHJ1ZX0%3D

OPERA America. (2024b). Racial Justice Opera Forum 2024. https://tickettailor.com/events/operaamerica/1141803?a=OANONMEMBER23

OPERA America. (2024c). Gender Parity. https://operaamerica.org/industry-resources/#eyJxIjoiIiwidG9waWNzIjpbMjIzM10sImNvbnRlbnRUeXBlcyI6W10sImlzc3VlIjowLCJlZGl0b3JQaWNrIjpmYWxzZSwicHJvZ3JhbX-MiOmZhbHNlLCJleHBsb3JlIjpmYWxzZSwic29ydCI6MCwiZnJvbSI6b-nVsbCwidG8iOm51bGwsInBhZ2UiOjEsInBhZ2VTaXplIjoyNCwidmll-dyI6MSwibWFnUGFnZSI6MSwibWFnUGFnZVNpemUiOjI0LCJtYWd-hemluZSI6ZmFsc2UsImxvYWRUb3BpY1BpbnMiOnRydWV9

OPERA America. (2024d). Racial Justice. https://operaamerica.org/industry-resources/#eyJxIjoiIiwidG9waWNzIjpbMjIzNF0sImNvbnRlbnRUeXBlcyI6W10sImlzc3VlIjowLCJlZGl0b3JQaWNrIjpmYWxzZSwicHJvZ3JhbX-MiOmZhbHNlLCJleHBsb3JlIjpmYWxzZSwic29ydCI6MCwiZnJvbSI6b-nVsbCwidG8iOm51bGwsInBhZ2UiOjEsInBhZ2VTaXplIjoyNCwidmll-dyI6MSwibWFnUGFnZSI6MSwibWFnUGFnZVNpemUiOjI0LCJtYWd-hemluZSI6ZmFsc2UsImxvYWRUb3BpY1BpbnMiOnRydWV9

Price, A., & Applebaum, L. (2022, September 30). A Free Survey to Measure a Sense of Belonging at Museums. https://aam-us.org/2022/09/30/a-free-survey-to-measure-a-sense-of-belonging-at-museums/?utm_source=American+Alliance+of+Museums&utm_campaign=40c290a1af-FieldNotes_2023_Sep11&utm_medium=email&utm_term=0_-40c290a1af-%5BLIST_EMAIL_ID%5D

Rose, V. (2021). ACF Artist Equity Summit Recap and Equity Report Card. https://icareifyoulisten.com/2021/09/acf-artist-equity-summit-recap-equity-report-card/

San Francisco Opera. (2024). Community: Diversity, Equity and Community. https://sfopera.com/dec/

Sweeney, L., Harkins, D., & Dressel, J. (2022). Art Museum Staff Demographic Survey. https://sr.ithaka.org/wp-content/uploads/2022/11/Mellon-Art-Museum-Staff-Demographic-Survey-11162022.pdf

Telford, T., Felton, E., & Guskin, E. (2024, June 18). Most Americans Approve of DEI, According to Post-Ipsos Poll. *The Washington Post*. https://washingtonpost.com/nation/2024/06/18/affirmative-action-dei-attiudes-poll/?utm_campaign=wp_post_most&utm_medium=email&utm_source=newsletter&wpisrc=nl_most&carta-url=https%3A%2F%2Fs2.washingtonpost.com%2Fcar-ln-tr%2F3e07dd0%2F6671af4b00d189674ce4a1ac%2F610045b5ade4e20d1441668b%2F20%2F52%2F6671af4b00d189674ce4a1ac

Woods, S. (2024, July 19). Forward Thinking: Culture Matters. *Symphony*. https://symphony.org/features/forward-thinking-culture-matters/

5 Conclusion

Where Might the U.S. Creative Sector Go from Here?

As a reminder, in Chapter 1, I described the cultural, historical, political, and social contexts in which the U.S. creative sector exists. I argued that an obsession with power enables the ways in which U.S. society socializes people to its context by placing them into the *Matrix of Caste in the U.S.* based on devalued and valued social identities. I also reflected on DEI's aim to shift the U.S. away from caste as a mode of operandi to a pluralist democracy that fully enables the flourishing of all humans, regardless of their social identities. Lastly, I discussed the importance of eradicating caste within the creative sector, described my positionality, and closed the chapter with a definition of key terms used throughout this book.

I posed ADEI and *creative justice* as *a* solution to address the enduring wicked problem of caste within the U.S. creative sector in Chapter 2. I also further defined ADEI, theorized the relationships that exist between the short-term goals and practices, and described their relationships to *creative justice*. Lastly, I argued that ADEI should facilitate *creative justice*, the long-term goal for which the creative sector should aim to achieve.

In Chapter 3, I operationalized the theory of *creative justice* introduced in Chapter 2. I presented the Creative Justice Procedural Model, which described the systematic steps by which ADEI leads to *creative justice*. I also posed five questions to help cultural organizations interrogate their short-term goals and practice of ADEI to improve their strategies for achieving *creative justice*. These questions included: (1) To what extent has the creative sector removed barriers to participation **with** historically and continuously low casted peoples? (2) To what extent has the creative sector intentionally engaged **with** historically and continuously low casted peoples? (3) To what extent has the creative sector addressed historic, continuous, and long-suffered unfairness **with** historically and continuously low casted peoples through policies and practices? (4) To what extent has the creative sector created belonging **with** historically and continuously low casted peoples? And (5) what are the implications for the creative sector if it does not address caste **with** historically and continuously low casted peoples?

DOI: 10.4324/9781003246909-5

I examined the AAM, ACF, Chorus America, League of American Orchestras, and OPERA America's use of ADEI to improve their climate, culture, and intentional engagement with people across the vastness of human differences toward *creative justice* in Chapter 4. I also briefly described the YOSA's work tackling adultism to actualize a creative third place for young people. In addition, I offered the Dance Data Project's *Gender Equity Index* and Kathy Hsieh's *Continuum on Becoming an Anti-Racist Arts and Cultural Organization* as tools that can assist cultural organizations in improving their climate and culture to advance *creative justice*.

In this final chapter, I interrogate current attacks on and criticisms of DEI. I suggest a research agenda that practitioners and scholars should partner in investigating to affirm, conceptualize, and identify effective evidence-based approaches for advancing and manifesting *creative justice* in the U.S. creative sector. Lastly, I reflect on the implications for the creative sector if it does not develop a code of ethics that will guide sectoral-wide transformation in pursuit of dismantling and eradicating caste toward *creative justice*.

Diversity, Equity, and Inclusion in the U.S.: A Status Update

As practices, DEI has become increasingly professionalized since the Civil Rights movement. From a purely economic perspective, one estimate valuated the DEI industry at $3.4 billion in 2020 (Signal, 2023), while another estimated the DEI industry's value at $7.5 billion with an expectation to double to $15.4 billion by 2026 (Navagant, 2023). Demand for DEI, or ADEI as I have called it throughout this book, increased in the creative sector since 2020 after the convicted felon, Derek Chauvin, murdered George Floyd. However, with the increasing professionalization of DEI as an intervention for combating systemic caste and the avarice for power that it enables has also come critiques of the practices for under-delivering on their aims. Diversity training, especially, has received a great deal of critiques for its lack of efficacy at eliminating caste (Dobbin & Kaleve, 2018; Paluck, 2022; Singal, 2023).

In addition to questioning the merit of mandatory training, some question the practice of villainizing dominant or high casted groups, while simultaneously further victimizing low casted groups. Dobbin and Kaleve (2018) contended that two common features of diversity training, mandatory participation and legal curriculum, make participants feel controlled by an external power. Asare (2022) also argued that DEI training often centers its effects on high casted groups, while under-interrogating the impacts of training on historically and continuously low casted groups.

Furthermore, Patel (2023) and Appiah (2019) proposed that DEI focuses too much on power, privilege, and oppression. But, given that caste and its wicked outcomes have been so deeply rooted in and throughout U.S. society is it reasonable to expect nearly 60 years of somewhat of a course correct to completely eradicate or even reduce 400+ years of brutality, cruelty, and unnecessary human suffering? How can U.S. society actualize cooperation and a peaceful co-existence of people when it has historically and continuously socialized some people to internalize inferiority and/or superiority to other people? Furthermore, how can people learn to live together when society socializes some people to believe that they have a right to rule over people low casted, othered, and subalterned by devalued social identities in U.S. society? Though disagreement abounds on the philosophical, practical, technical, and theoretical underpinnings of DEI, the practices have shown promise in aiding the U.S.' transformation toward a thriving pluralist democracy. Still, some politicians have disingenuously weaponized DEI's critiques with efficiency and impactful consequences for education, employment, healthcare, and philanthropy, among other areas critical to peoples' material lives.

According to the Chronicle of Higher Education's DEI Legislation Tracker, which has tracked changes on several college campuses in 29 states, policymakers have introduced 126 anti-DEI bills that would prohibit colleges and universities from having DEI offices and staff, banned mandatory DEI training, prohibited institutions from using DEI statements in hiring and promotion, and prohibited colleges from using race, sex, color, ethnicity, or national origin in admissions or employment (Chronicle of Higher Education, 2024). Though governors have only signed 14 of the proposed bills into law and tabled 53 (likely until after the 2024 Presidential Election), the anti-DEI movement has effectively constrained higher education's ability and espoused commitment to upend systemic caste in higher education, which has cost the U.S. economy $956 billion annually according to Carnevale et al. (2021). The SCOTUS also enabled attacks against DEI by banning affirmative action in college admissions at elite universities (Associated Press, 2023).

The Republicans' smear campaign against affirmative action has long caused enduring misunderstandings about the policy's true aims in U.S. society. The policy never intended to give *unqualified* Black and other historically and continuously low casted peoples opportunities over qualified people from high casted groups (able-bodied, White, Christian, cisgender, heterosexual, and male). Affirmative action aimed to give **qualified** Black and other historically and continuously low casted peoples access to the same opportunities as qualified people from high casted groups. Affirmative action, aided by DEI, somewhat succeeded in leveling the playing field to equal opportunity by encouraging real competition for opportunities among diverse peoples (cuyler, 2013). But a minority of high casted peoples who fear losing and sharing power and privilege aim to halt any further progress made at enabling human flourishing despite social identity. This includes progress made in corporations (Telford, 2023), though corporations fought back when President Reagan tried to undo affirmative action in the 1980s (Mark, 2024a) and in and through philanthropy (Daniels, 2023a, 2023b; Herschander, 2023). Simultaneously, some historically and continuously low casted groups and their accomplices and allies critique DEI for not going far enough in achieving more progress (Newkirk, 2019).

Though conservative activists and state attorney generals in Republican-led states feel emboldened to launch attacks on DEI because the SCOTUS banned affirmative action in college admissions (Chronicle of Higher Education, 2024; Jones, 2024), specifically targeting corporations (Telford, 2023), government (Mark, 2023), museums (Mark, 2024b) and other cultural organizations (cuyler, 2023), nonprofits (Chronicle of Philanthropy, 2023), and philanthropy (Daniels, 2023a, 2023b; Herschander, 2023), state attorney generals in Democrat-led states appear poised for an impending legal war (Telford, 2023). In fact, this group of state attorneys encouraged and provided corporations with guidance on how to continue their DEI-related work (Ford et al., 2023). In addition, Confessore's (2024) exposé on the anti-DEI movement for the *New York Times* made it clear that a fear of competition, a desire to constrain human flourishing, lust for power and privilege, and willingness to undermine a peaceful co-existence among humans motivate the irrational crusade against DEI. I consider it poetic that the anti-DEI movement continues its crusade at its own peril.

According to a poll in June of 2024, most U.S. citizens (60%) approved of DEI, and that number increased to 69% for programs such as internships for low casted groups and anti-bias training, especially when including a specific definition. However, financial incentives for managers who achieve diversity remained universally unpopular (Telford et al., 2024). If the Honorable Elijah Cummings' comment in 2016 that, "Diversity is not our problem . . . it's our promise because it allows us to live by our democratic ideals of fairness and equality" (League of American Orchestras, 2024) at the League of American Orchestras conference is true, then anti-DEI actions, behaviors, laws, policies, and practices will cause an increase in discrimination lawsuits, revealing that improving DEI interventions remain more affordable and desirable than avoidable and costly lawsuits (League of American Orchestras, 2024).

In addition, to refine DEI, Dobbin and Kaleve (2018) suggested that corporations and organizations improve the effects of training by making it part of a wider program of change. Asare (2022) supported this idea and advocated for avoiding 'check box' thinking in DEI and examining the impacts of training through a more expansive and nuanced lens. Appiah (2019) explicitly argued that cooperation, cosmopolitanism, and focusing on building a healthy and diverse democracy would make a better approach to DEI. To eradicate workplace harm due to systemic caste, DEI educators and facilitators should plan their curricula more intentionally and sequentially. As I have advocated throughout this book, add access to diversity, equity, and inclusion to enable a process that systematically enables ADEI and *creative justice* (cuyler, 2023). The creative sector and the cultural organizations that comprise it should also use evidence-based approaches to ADEI, while maintaining an anti-caste ethos and practice that aims to eradicate discrimination, exclusion, marginalization, oppression, othering, subalterning, and subjugation. I also encourage cultural organizations to develop a 'culture of care' by centering concern for the planet and people, especially through the lens of well-being (Woods, 2024). When people believe that their places of employment truly 'care' about them, it enhances their loyalty and performance. Lastly, advocacy for organizational transformation leadership and management must also inform the creative sector's use of ADEI to advance and manifest *creative justice*. But the creative sector should also seek to learn more.

From ADEI to Manifesting Creative Justice: A Research Agenda

Historically, the U.S. government has not consistently or largely designed cultural policies with the *creative justice* of people with disabilities, people of the global majority, immigrants, LGBTQ+ people, low socio-economic status, nonbinary, women, young people, or any other devalued social identities in mind. This policy and practice gap has created a remarkable opportunity for scholars to advance empirical and theoretical discourses that will advance, inform, and enhance the pursuit of *creative justice* for all historically and continuously low casted peoples in the U.S. In Chapter 4, I revealed a list of ADEI interventions that cultural organizations have used to advance, facilitate, and manifest *creative justice*.

The list included accreditation, hiring ADEI professionals, affinity groups, and annual reporting on ADEI success and opportunities; assessment, evaluation, and research; budgetary allocations, education/professional development, digital educational resources, and funding and grant opportunities; and strategic planning. Researchers should investigate which of these interventions yields the greatest return on investment for cultural organizations qualitatively and quantitatively. In addition, researchers should investigate the efficacy of cultural organizations using diverse affinity groups to tackle key caste-related problems. For example, how might a mixed-gender "pay equity" affinity group within a cultural organization address pay inequity? Or a similarly comprised affinity group designed to advise cultural organizations on when, how, and why to make political statements, or not.

Though a poll found that U.S. citizens do not support financial incentives for managers who achieve diversity (Telford, Felton, & Guskin, 2024), I am curious to know what would happen if cultural organizations gave their employees autonomy to choose aspects of its *creative justice* work to lead and manage, while holding them accountable for accomplishing and completing such tasks through their annual evaluations. Thus, an experimental design study might reveal a new intervention that reminds all employees of the cultural organization that everyone has some responsibility for achieving *creative justice* through climate, culture, and intentional engagement with the vastness of human difference; and that show the veracity of an intervention not broadly used in cultural organizations. Furthermore, the following list includes broad, empirical, philosophical, pragmatic, specific, and theoretical research questions that scholars could partner with practitioners in investigating in future research on *creative justice*:

1. In what ways does the creative sector engage in caste and the discrimination, exclusion, marginalization, oppression, othering, subalterning, and subjugation that it produces?
2. In what ways have cultural policies addressed and/or perpetuated creative *in*justice for low casted peoples in the U.S. creative sector?
3. What effects has caste had on the U.S. creative economy?
4. What differences exist in performance between cultural organizations that use ADEI to enable *creative justice* and those that do not?
5. For cultural organizations that begin and abandon ADEI, what do they learn and hold on to relative to *creative justice*?
6. What benefits have cultural organizations gained from prioritizing a 'culture of care' in pursuit of *creative justice*?
7. In what ways do artistic and cultural products enable *creative justice*?
8. In what ways have cultural organizations used ADEI as strategic transformation leadership and management?
9. What role should arts leaders play in addressing creative *in*justice *with* historically and continuously low casted peoples in society?
10. How can *creative justice* inform cultural policies related to the return of cultural objects acquired due to armed conflict, colonialism, expansionism, and imperialism?
11. Is it possible to disentangle arts entrepreneurship, leadership, management, and cultural policy education and practice from its caste-based, colonialist, expansionist, hegemonic, imperialist, patriarchal, racist, and White supremacist origins?
12. In what ways could framing arts entrepreneurship, leadership, management, and cultural policy studies through the lens of *creative justice* improve teaching and learning in these academic disciplines?
13. In what ways does humanity benefit from *creative justice*?

While scholars should not consider these questions prescriptive, they should see these research questions as suggestive of an emerging research agenda that can add meaning, significance, and value to arts entrepreneurship, leadership, management, and cultural policy education, practice, and research. I also hope that these questions inspire additional research questions that I have not expressed here. Ultimately, I aspire to incite transformational thought about the discipline's efforts to de-colonize arts entrepreneurship, leadership, management, and cultural policy education, practice, and research. If practitioners and scholars truly understand cultural policy as corporations', governments', individuals', and institutions' constraining or enabling of cultural engagement, flourishing, practices, and values, then all cultural workers have a social responsibility to use ADEI to address creative *in*justice within the creative sector.

Where Does the U.S. Creative Sector Go from Here?

Throughout this book, I aimed to make the case for combatting caste and the creative *in*justice it enables within the U.S. creative sector. Personally, experiencing and observing identity-based human suffering has compelled me to wonder, is identity-based human suffering absolutely necessary? If so, what is the return on the investment in human suffering? Nevertheless, the ways in which identity-based human suffering constrains human flourishing deeply troubles me, especially within the creative sector. I often contemplate the artistic and creative harm that the Curtis Institute of Music perpetrated on Nina Simone by denying her admission to study classical piano because of her race. The League of American Orchestras' (2020) *Statement on Racial Discrimination*, too, made a similar argument stating, "the impacts of our actions have included *the loss of valuable musical and other creative contributions by generations of Black people*". To have one's artistic and creative flourishing constrained, not for a lack of ability, expertise, skill, and/or talent, but for some unmitigable characteristic is asinine, cruel, and insidious. It also compels me to consider a quote attributed to St. Thomas Aquinas, "If you can live amid injustice without anger, you are immoral and unjust" from *The Summa Theologica* (Aquinas, 1274). Yet, if an infinite number of low casted peoples have had their artistic and creative flourishing constrained by devalued social identities due to caste, what has, and will it continue to cost humanity?

Keller (1989) argued, "an inequity in cultural power in our system results in losses of opportunity for public sharing, critical understanding, and acceptance of art". I have argued previously, and still believe, that if the creative sector does not address creative *in*justice the U.S. and humanity writ large will suffer irreversible and grave artistic, creative, and cultural deficits (cuyler, 2019). Still, if laws, policies, practices, loss of revenue, and loss of remarkable talent has not been enough of a deterrent, what might compel the U.S. creative sector's transformation toward *creative justice*?

In 2022, Abruzzo argued that the arts needed a code of ethics. He cited several concerns across the creative sector among them museums' repatriation of ill-acquired cultural objects, deaccessioning of art in museums, tainted donations, and #BLM and #MeToo, to name a few rationales for developing a code of ethics. Inspired by Abruzzo's (2022) article, I participated in a group that attempted to draft a code of ethics. However, drafting the code of ethics proved more difficult than the group anticipated.

Though the Association of Arts Administration Educators' Standards for Graduate and Undergraduate Curricula mention the words ethical (21/14), ethics (2), and ethically (1) (Association of Arts Administration Educators, 2014, 2018), students receive too little education on and few opportunities to practice ethical arts leadership. Furthermore, the standards do not articulate the necessity of an *Ethical Arts Leadership* course. As a result, I added such a course to my teaching portfolio at the University of Michigan. In the first two iterations of the course, as the final, I required my students to asynchronously and collaboratively write a Code of Ethics based on their semester's long learning. My students continue to impress me with their work so much so that in April 2024, I partnered with colleagues at the University of Music and Performing Arts in Vienna to present a convening entitled, *Critiques of Power in the Arts*. The week of the convening my colleagues and I facilitated sessions for students as a part of a Global Classroom where some of the students presented their Code of Ethics and their process for developing their code.

Unfortunately, whether intentionally or not, some of the attendees misunderstood that the students intended for the global convening to adopt their Code of Ethics, rather than that the students simply wanted to share their process for developing their Code of Ethics in hopes that it would spark dialogue and action toward developing a Code of Ethics for the global creative sector. Reflecting on the experience, several questions emerged for me including: (1) For what reason do we need to critique power in the arts, especially when power has not abused or misused itself, humans have? (2) Does the global and U.S. creative sectors need a Code of Ethics or a Moral Code that will guide the treatment of humans in and above laws? (3) If so, why? (4) If so, who has and should have the power to write and enforce a Code of Ethics? (5) If the creative sector articulates profound reasons for developing a Code of Ethics, but do not, does it compromise the creative sector's moral authority and capital? Furthermore, what moral injury might the global creative sector suffer by not doing so? Lastly, (6) if accountants, doctors, and lawyers take their professions seriously enough to develop Codes of Ethics, why does the creative sector resist doing the same given that cultural organizations and the workers that they employ often lack a clear ethos and practice of moral management (Keller, 1989)?

Far too often, the creative sector shrinks away from its ethical and moral obligation and social responsibility to the public. As I argued in Chapter 3, the creative sector should practice ADEI to achieve *creative justice* because (1) it is the right thing to do, (2) their missions should compel them to do so, as does (3) their nonprofit status, and (4) economics. However, the creative sector has prioritized its relationships with elite and wealthy major donors further entrenching a "socioeconomically stratified cultural order that perpetuates inequity" (Keller, 1989) to the detriment of the public to whom the creative sector should primarily remain beholden. Indeed, nonprofit status affords the creative sector tax exemption, which saves cultural organizations an unvaluated amount of money, except for on unrelated business income (UBI). In addition, nonprofit status enables the philanthropic ecosystem that rewards corporations, foundations, and individuals for contributing with a reduction in their taxes, too. Lastly, city, county, state, regional, and the national government provide direct funding to the creative sector. But what if the creative sector could do both? I hypothesize, supported by Becker (1971), that doing the right thing, optimizing its moral capital would bolster the creative sector's contributed and earned revenue. In fact, when my clients have asked, "should we continue our ADEI work or develop a COVID-19 recovery strategy?" I have responded, "what if practicing ADEI, especially with the aim of achieving *creative justice*, is your COVID-19 recovery strategy?"

In the name of beauty and entertainment, I fear that some people within the creative sector will continue weaponizing 'artistic excellence' and 'artistic merit' as excuses to avoid practicing ADEI to achieve *creative justice* hiding from the sector's ethical and moral responsibility in how it treats people. Is it asking too much that the creative sector presents and produces 'artistic excellence' and 'artistic merit' as humanely as possible? Surely, the creative sector cannot truly believe that it can only achieve 'artistic excellence' and 'artistic merit' through profound identity-based human suffering. If so, then survivors of reported sexual abuse in the creative sector admonished, "artistic merit, while significant, should not take precedence over issues of moral injury and human dignity" (Awuah-Darko, 2024). Alas, the barbarity and tyranny of caste constrains individual rights and human flourishing. It also erodes and threatens civilization, social cohesion, and a peaceful co-existence among humans. After all, what would a demagogue exploit without caste-enabled social divisions? Given its powers of creativity and innovation, the U.S. creative sector should take a more decisive and proactive role in ensuring and protecting the *creative justice* of all low casted peoples. As Keller (1989) argued, "It is unacceptable, whether through innocent negligence or knowing complicity, to impede the access of those whose artistic and cultural promise remains yet unfulfilled". Indeed, because being creative is as indigenous to being human as is breathing.

References

Abruzzo, J. (2022, January 29). The Arts Need a Code of Ethics. *LinkedIn.* https://linkedin.com/pulse/arts-need-code-ethics-james-abruzzo?trk=articles_directory

Appiah, K. (2019). *The Lies That Bind: Rethinking Identity.* Liveright Publishing Corporation.

Aquinas, T. (1274). *The "Summa Theologica."* Benziger Brother.

Asare, J. (2022, October 7). Have We Been Wrongfully Vilifying DEI Training? *Forbes.* https://forbes.com/sites/janicegassam/2022/10/07/have-we-been-wrongfully-vilifying-dei-training/?sh=4af908d53b35

Associated Press. (2023, July 1). Recent U.S. Supreme Court Rulings: What You Need to Know. https://voanews.com/a/recent-us-supreme-court-rulings-what-you-need-to-know-/7162909.html

Association of Arts Administration Educators. (2014). Standards for Arts Administration Graduate Program Curricula: A Living Document. https://artsadministration.org/new-aaae-graduate-standards/

Association of Arts Administration Educators. (2018). Standards for Arts Administration Undergraduate Curricula: A Living Document.

Awuah-Darko, J. (2024). Victims Urge the NCAC and Cultural Institutions to Push for Investigations of Claims Against Kehinde Wiley. https://hyperallergic.com/929429/kehinde-wileys-accusers-respond-to-concerns-over-canceled-museum-shows/

Becker, G. (1971). *The Economics of Discrimination*, 2nd Ed. University of Chicago Press.

Carnevale, A., Campbell, K., Cheah, B., Fasules, M., Gulish, A., Quinn, M., Sablan, J., Smith, N., Strohl, J., & Barrese, S. (2021). The Cost of Economic and Racial Injustice in Postsecondary Education. https://cew.georgetown.edu/wp-content/uploads/cew-the-cost-of-economic-and-racial-injustice.pdf

Chronicle of Higher Education. (2024). DEI Legislation Tracker. https://www-chronicle-com.proxy.lib.umich.edu/article/here-are-the-states-where-lawmakers-are-seeking-to-ban-colleges-dei-efforts

Chronicle of Philanthropy. (2023, August 10). How the Supreme Court Ruling on Race Affects Nonprofits and Foundations. https://philanthropy.com/events/virtual/online-briefing/how-the-supreme-court-ruling-on-race-affects-nonprofits-and-foundations

Confessore, N. (2024, January 20). 'America Is Under Attack': Inside the Anti-DEI Crusade. *The New York Times*. https://nytimes.com/interactive/2024/01/20/us/dei-woke-claremont-institute.html

cuyler, a. c. (2013). Affirmative Action and Diversity: Implications for Arts Management. *Journal of Arts Management, Law, and Society*, *43*(2), pp. 98–105.

cuyler, a. c. (2019). The Role of Foundations in Achieving Creative Justice in the U.S. Cultural Sector. *Grantmakers in the Arts Reader*, *30*(1), p. 6.

cuyler, a. c. (2023). Access, Diversity, Equity, and Inclusion (ADEI) in Cultural Organizations: Challenges and Opportunities. In A. Rhine & J. Pension (Eds.), *Business Issues in the Arts* (pp. 83–104). Routledge.

Daniels, A. (2023a, December 13). Grantmaking Groups Stand Firm in Defense of Race-Based Philanthropy. *The Chronicle of Philanthropy*. https://philanthropy.com/article/grant-making-groups-stand-firm-in-defense-of-race-based-philanthropy?utm_source=Iterable&utm_medium=email&utm_campaign=campaign_8536414_nl_Philanthropy-Today_date_20231213&cid=pt&source=&sourceid=&sra=true

Daniels, C. (2023b, December 20). A Post Affirmative Action World Demands More-Not Less- Funding for Black Leaders. *The Chronicle of Philanthropy*. https://philanthropy.com/article/a-post-affirmative-action-world-demands-more-not-less-funding-for-black-leaders?utm_source=Iterable&utm_medium=email&utm_campaign=campaign_8598271_nl_Philanthropy-Today_date_20231220&cid=pt&source=&sourceid=&sra=true

Dobbin, F., & Kalev, A. (2018). Why Doesn't Diversity Training Work? *Anthropology Now*, *10*(2), pp. 48–55.

Ford, A., Newby, C., Brady, C., Benitez-Thompson, T., Prio, L., & Stern, H. (2023, July 19). Letter to Fortune 100 CEOs. https://illinoisattorneygeneral.gov/News-Room/Current-News/Fortune%20100%20Letter%20-%20FINAL.pdf

Herschander, S. (2023, December 15). Despite Momentum, Many Nonprofits Struggle With Basic Dei Principles. *The Chronicle of Philanthropy*. https://philanthropy.com/article/despite-momentum-many-nonprofits-still-struggle-with-basic-dei-principles?utm_source=Iterable&utm_medium=email&utm_campaign=campaign_8558178_nl_Philanthropy-Today_date_20231215&cid=pt&source=&sourceid=&sra=true

Jones, S. (2024). The War on DEI Is About Hierarchy. *Intelligencer*. https://msn.com/en-us/news/opinion/the-war-on-dei-is-about-hierarchy/ar-BB1h8UpL?ocid=mailsignout&pc=U591&cvid=73810af743f6490097515adce8c98091&ei=30

Keller, A. (1989). The Arts Manager's Social Responsibility. *Journal of Arts Management, Law, and Society*, *19*(2), pp. 44–54.

League of American Orchestras. (2020). *Statement on Racial Discrimination*. https://americanorchestras.org/a-new-statement-on-racial-discrimination-august-2020/

League of American Orchestras. (2024). Making the Case for Equity, Diversity, and Inclusion in Orchestras: A Guide from the League of American Orchestras. https://americanorchestras.org/making-the-case-for-equity-diversity-and-inclusion-in-orchestras/

Mark, J. (2023, September 7). SBA Program Upended in Wake of Supreme Court Affirmative Action Ruling. *The Washington Post*. https://washingtonpost.com/business/2023/09/07/sba-8a-program-ruling-affirmative-action/

Mark, J. (2024a, January 21). When Regan Tried to Undo Affirmative Action, Corporations Fought Back. *The Washington Post*. https://washingtonpost.com/history/2024/01/21/ronald-reagan-affirmative-action-dei/

Mark, J. (2024b, March 27). Smithsonian's Latino Museum Settles With Affirmative Action Foe. *The Washington Post*. https://washingtonpost.com/business/2024/03/27/smithsonian-latino-museum-settlement/

Navagant. (2023). Demand for Diversity, Equity, and Inclusion Solutions on the Rise. https://navagant.com/wp-content/uploads/2023/08/Navagant_Diversity-Equity-Inclusion-Solutions-Industry-Report-Q3-2023.pdf

Newkirk, P. (2019). *Diversity, Inc.: The Failed Promise of a Billion-Dollar Business*. Bold Type Books.

Paluck, B. (2022, December 12). Does diversity training work? We don't know, and some CEOs don't want to. *The Washington Post*. https://www.washingtonpost.com/opinions/2022/12/12/diversity-training-effectiveness-psychologist/

Patel, E. (2023, September 6). Today's DEI Is Obsessed With Power and Privilege: It's Time to Overturn the Robin DiAngelo and Ibram X. Kendi Model. *The Chronicle of Higher Education*. https://www-chronicle-com.proxy.lib.umich.edu/article/todays-dei-is-obsessed-with-power-and-privilege

Singal, J. (2023, January 17). What If Diversity Training Is Doing More Harm Than Good? *The New York Times*. https://nytimes.com/2023/01/17/opinion/dei-trainings-effective.html

Telford, T. (2023, December 27). 2024 Might be Do-Or-Die for Corporate Diversity Efforts. Here's Why. *The Washington Post*. https://washingtonpost.com/business/2023/12/27/dei-affirmative-action-legal-challenges-corporate-america/?utm_campaign=wp_post_most&utm_medium=email&utm_source=newsletter&wpisrc=nl_most

Woods, S. (2024, July 19). Forward Thinking: Culture Matters. *Symphony*. https://symphony.org/features/forward-thinking-culture-matters/

Index

Note: Page numbers in *italics* indicate a figure and page numbers in **bold** indicate a table on the corresponding page.

For Product Safety Concerns and Information please contact our EU representative GPSR@taylorandfrancis.com
Taylor & Francis Verlag GmbH, Kaufingerstraße 24, 80331 München, Germany

www.ingramcontent.com/pod-product-compliance
Ingram Content Group UK Ltd.
Pitfield, Milton Keynes, MK11 3LW, UK
UKHW021245190926
475569UK00001BA/19
* 9 7 8 1 0 3 2 1 6 0 5 3 5 *